GOD'S AD-MAN

Tom Glynn

Ark House Press
PO Box 1722, Port Orchard, WA 98366 USA
PO Box 1321, Mona Vale NSW 1660 Australia
PO Box 318 334, West Harbour, Auckland 0661 New Zealand
arkhousepress.com

© 2021 Tom Glynn

Scripture quotations taken from The Holy Bible, New International Version® NIV®. Copyright © 1973 1978 1984 2011 by Biblica, Inc. TM. Used by permission.

Scripture quotations also taken from the New King James Version®. Copyright © 1982 by Thomas Nelson. Used by permission. All rights reserved.

All rights reserved. No part of this publication may be reproduced, stored in a retrieval system or transmitted in any form or by any means electronic, mechanical, photocopying, recording or otherwise without the prior written permission of the publisher.

Cataloguing in Publication Data:
Title: God's Ad-Man
ISBN: 978-0-6451417-4-0 (pbk)
Subjects: Biography; Business; Marketing; Christians in Business;
Other Authors/Contributors: Glynn, Tom

Cover and Photo Insert designed by Craig Woodhead and typeset by initiateagency.com

For my family with love and gratitude.

CONTENTS

Acknowledgements vii
Introduction ix
1. The Beginning 1
2. A Happy Childhood 9
3. The Taste Of Failure 21
4. Advertising Here I Come 27
5. My First Business 33
6. Rising 39
7. God And Glynn 49
8. Converted 57
9. Singapore - Colonial Style 63
10. Singapore On The Move 71
11. London Swings 81
12. Lynda 89
13. Leaving London 99
14. Home 105
15. How Advertising Works 111
16. Feminism And Film Stars 119
17. Tom Glynn Advertising (TGA) 127
18. Dream Fulfilled 133
19. Controversy 141

20.	Liberace Plays - TGA Soars	149
21.	Dealing With The Black Dog	155
22.	Learning About Depression	163
23.	Keeping Going	171
24.	TGA Sold	177
25.	On My Own	183
26.	Church Gypsies	189
27.	Another Opportunity	197
28.	Fame - A New Concept	205
29.	You Can't Win Them All	211
30.	My Two Selves	215
31.	Pluses And Minuses	221
32.	Man Alive	229
33.	God's Raindrops From Heaven	235
34.	The Glynn Tribe	243
35.	Family Matters	249
36.	A Church Grows	257
37.	'Get Up' And 'Speak Out'	265
38.	Now What?	269

APPENDIX 1: *Agencies and Clients* 277
APPENDIX 2: *TGA Worked With These Christian Organisations* 279
APPENDIX 3: *Spirited Australian Speakers* 281

ACKNOWLEDGEMENTS

Although I worked in advertising agencies, I did not see myself as a writer. I had talented people around me to write presentations, press releases and copy for ads etc. Thus I am grateful to my editors, Lynn Goldsmith, Sue Ellen Smith, Bruce Miller and Cecily Peterson. Thanks particuarly to an old friend and author, Rev David Nicholas who encouraged me to write this memoir and provided some of the chapter headings. Sadly David died in late 2020.

Also thanks to Hugh Mackay for writing extra copy for the chapter on 'How Advertising Works', and my psychiatrist who provided valuable insight about my depression.

I especially want to thank my wife, Lynda, who struggled to make sense of my poorly written scrawl and typed the first draft; and my son Stephen and daughter Amanda for helping with the different files. Thanks to Craig Woodhead, art director and long-time friend for his cover design.

Finally, thanks to my God, His son Jesus, and the Holy Spirit who have been my rock and guide over many years.

INTRODUCTION

How did the son of an illegal SP bookmaker, who failed to complete school, enter advertising? How did success eventually come from working in leading advertising agencies in Sydney, Singapore and London; and helping countless Christian groups to become more effective in raising funds and communicating the Christian Faith?

And all of this while struggling with clinical depression!

My career, throughout a major part of my life, was in advertising. I ran my own advertising agency in Sydney and, for the greater portion of my time as a business owner, it was rewarding work. I was drawn to advertising, having been influenced by my older brother Bruce, and with great enthusiasm and some talent I was fairly successful.

It all started in 1957 when I turned sixteen. This was the beginning of a long and satisfying career, although very tough at times.

I described myself as 'God's Ad-Man'. I did this honestly, and humbly, while hopefully not on an ego trip.

Working in advertising agencies can be glamorous, rewarding and extremely competitive. It's also a very difficult and challenging business. Agencies come and go. Giant international agency names no longer exist. Agencies succeed by servicing clients (called accounts). It doesn't cost a lot to open an advertising agency; what is needed is at least one client who has enough money to spend in advertising, giving the agency enough income to continue.

Two recent television shows have exposed what goes on behind the scenes in advertising agencies. One was the American series, *Mad Men*, named after the self-referential slang term coined in the 1950s by advertising agencies working in Madison Avenue, the New York mecca for advertising agencies. The other series is the ABC's *Gruen Transfer*, which refers to the response to designed disorientation in a retail environment. These TV series have helped attract young people to the sometimes glamorous worlds of advertising and public relations.

In my early twenties I became a Christian. If working in advertising agencies is tough, being a Christian in advertising is even tougher. This is particularly true in the situation where Christianity and the Church, in secular Australia, are often seen as negative and old-fashioned.

Life in ad agencies with some creative and senior executives was often based on long, boozy lunches, heavy drinking, sexual encounters and, in later years, drug taking. The commercial world of free enterprise, unbridled capitalism and materialism, and the teachings of Jesus Christ, were a little like chalk and cheese. The few Christians in advertising kept their Faith and beliefs to themselves.

This is my story of successes, failures, commitment and hope, in both my business and personal life.

Tom Glynn

'You can't go back and change the beginning,
but you can start where you are
and change the ending.'
C. S. LEWIS

CHAPTER 1

THE BEGINNING

I made a grand entrance into the world on 11 August 1941 at the recently opened King George V Memorial Hospital for Mothers and Babies in Camperdown, Sydney. I was one of the first ten babies born there. I was a war baby and I arrived one month prematurely. I was unfortunate to be born with a hernia and the surgeon had to operate on me at that early stage of my life. When I was strong enough to leave the hospital, I was taken home and my brother Bruce, who was eleven years older than me, carried me through the front door with my sister Dorothy, eight years older, proudly watching my arrival.

With Australia at war it was an uncertain time in history and to be alive. Four months after I was born, following Japan's attack on Pearl Harbour, America was at war with Japan and then with Germany, on 11 December 1941.

It's funny to think back on my very early years. Although I was in a family of five, the youngest of three children, it was, in many ways, like I was an only child with four parents - Mum, Dad, Bruce and Dorothy. The house I came home to, was in Majors Bay Road, Concord, which was then on the outskirts of the Sydney CBD, requiring a tram from Concord to Burwood railway station, then a train to the City.

Both Mum and Dad came from large families. My father, Thomas Malcolm, born in 1910, was the eldest of nine children. The youngest child, Richard, was born a year before my brother. As I say, a large family! My grandfather, also Thomas, was a quiet man with black hair. He didn't say much but sat in his chair overlooking Narrabeen Lakes. In his working life he was a barber at Camperdown and later at Willoughby. Grandma Glynn was the matriarch - extroverted, happy and very smart (she had to be because of her large family). Most of the Glynn family - my aunts and uncles - lived well into their seventies. Grandma and Grandpop Glynn bought a block of land on the corner of Pittwater Road and Lake Park Road, Narrabeen in the 50s. They lived in a tent and a garage until the house was built. Today it's a Jujitsu academy!

We didn't see a lot of the Glynns. With no car, it took about 90 minutes by public transport to travel from Concord to Narrabeen. Most of the married uncles and aunts moved to Collaroy Plateau, a newish nearby suburb. Sadly, when growing up, I didn't play with or see much of the large number of cousins.

Unfortunately, Mumma's family weren't as well off. But they were a large family, with six girls and one boy, Alfred. The girls were said to be stunning - a mixture of Scottish and Scandinavian stock. They all married well, except Madge, the most beautiful, who never married and sadly, became an alcoholic.

My maternal grandmother, Elsie Simpson, was born in Sydney shortly after the family arrived from Dundee, Scotland. My maternal grandfather, Alfred Anderson, died in his early

THE BEGINNING

thirties from pneumonia. It is believed he caught it from shielding his son, Alfred, from rain while they were travelling in a carriage in the early 1900s, returning from Cronulla Beach. Grandma Anderson became a sickly woman, possibly caused by the death of her husband and looking after seven children. Three of her daughters died in mid-life.

My father grew up in Buckingham Street, Surry Hills. He left school when he was fifteen, without any qualifications. He met Mum while working at the Bonds Clothing Factory in Camperdown, Sydney. (I would later work on the Bonds advertising account in the 1970s.) Dad and Mum were besotted with each other, and they married early in 1930. Their first child, my brother Bruce, was born in October of that year.

The economic depression made a huge impact on my parents - Dad couldn't find any work in Sydney. Having no qualifications didn't help. The impacts of the Great Depression were felt severely in Australia, with industrial unemployment rates exceeded only by Germany. One in three men didn't have a job, including my father.

To survive, the young family moved in with Grandma and Grandpop Glynn, and Dad's younger siblings, in the new garden suburb of Haberfield in western Sydney. It was a large Federation house with wide verandas. The house is still there today, but the pretty lead light windows have been replaced with aluminium windows. It was a tough time for the family. Mum would talk about how she walked five miles home because she had no money for a bus. Additionally, she and Grandma Glynn didn't get on well because there was friction caused by so many people living in the one house. Despite the many challenges, everyone survived through the difficult times and found their feet again. Of course, then, the next challenge was the War.

Unlike most men, Dad didn't go to war. We never knew why he didn't go to fight; he didn't tell us, and we never asked. It may have been because he had flat feet, or more likely because he worked at AWA at Five Dock, building essential parts for the war.

After the war, he was the manager of a billiard room with two pool tables, poker machines and card playing tables. In the back room, Dad was busy on the phone taking bets. This is called SP (Starting Prices) bookmaking, and it was illegal. The room was heavy with smoke and there were no windows, so that people outside were unable to see what was going on. There was also no outside sign advising what was going on inside.

These activities had to be kept very private, as there was always the chance that the police would come banging on the door and charge Dad with keeping a house of illegal gambling. He was very stressed when a high-ranking policeman moved to a house within walking distance from the premises. Fortunately, the police never called, and I have often wondered if he paid them to turn a blind eye. I never asked him and to this day I still have no idea.

Like most children, I don't remember a lot about my early years. When the Japanese midget submarines attacked Sydney Harbour from 31 May to 1 June 1942, I was told later that we huddled together in the hallway with the lights out. This was a wake-up call for many Sydneysiders, as they perceived the war to be far away and that they were somewhat immune from any attack.

THE BEGINNING

This attack was the second one. Darwin had been attacked on 19 February in the same year with two raids, the Japanese killing 235 people and wounding up to 400 people. Despite these attacks, WWII had little impact on me, although I was surprised to see camouflaged army trucks being driven around Sydney.

When the war ended, life continued on as normal for me… except for a health issue that would be with me for a long time.

> 'The childhood shows the man as morning shows the day.'
> JOHN MILTON

CHAPTER 2

A HAPPY CHILDHOOD

When I was about five or six I developed asthma, brought on by house dust and sudden changes in temperature. There were no 'puffers' in those days; the only treatment was to burn ground leaves. Mum would light the leaves in a saucer at my bedside; they would burn, sending up smoke for me to breathe to help clear my airways. Unfortunately, I had asthma off and on until my early twenties, until Ventolin became available, which helped me tremendously. I have not suffered with asthma since then.

Apart from the crushed leaves, the other treatment was a regular injection of an antibody. Mum and I would catch the number 461 bus, where I would scramble upstairs like a monkey to sit at the front of the double-decker bus. It would take about forty minutes to Missenden Road, Camperdown. From there we walked to the outpatients' section in the same hospital where I was born. We would sit on benches waiting to see the doctor and move along as the queue shortened. After an hour, I was ushered in to see the doctor, who injected me with a serum of house dust. With a sore arm, we would retreat to a café opposite for a soda and ice cream. That was a great treat after my injection. Asthma continued to be a worry and a nuisance. Another challenge was speaking: I did not pronounce words correctly, especially words starting with 's'. I also spoke too quickly and couldn't be understood. Mum would take me to a speech therapist at the Children's Hospital, Camperdown, where I would try to pronounce 's' successfully. The words of the poem the speech therapist had me practise stay with me today:

Three little ghosts
Sitting on posts
Eating buttered toast
Greasing their fists
Up to their wrists
Oh, what beasts
To make such feast.

During my career, I had difficulties speaking in public - understandably so, as in addition to my pronunciation problem, fear of public speaking is listed as one of the most common phobias after fear of dying. It's even higher than being hit by a car, meaning that people would rather be run over than give a speech. Today, I'm comfortable to speak and pray in public, often starting with 'I feel a speech or prayer coming on'.

I grew up in the 1940s - technically part of the Builder generation, although I came of age amongst the Baby Boomers. My wife, Lynda, born in 1946, was a Baby Boomer - one of the first. The '40s were a different world. America had become the world's leading power and its influence was everywhere. Some cars were imported from Detroit; large two-tone cars with fins that seemed to become larger and uglier each year. Labour saving domestic appliances had hit the stores, but there was no television, supermarkets, mobile phones, or internet. Most mothers stayed home looking after their children. Very few families had a car, including us. Our local grocer, opposite our house, would serve customers across the counter, where broken biscuits from the famous Arnott's tins could be bought for one penny.

Mum was a good cook. We had an 'Early Kooka' Metters gas stove, with the famous picture of a kookaburra and a worm on the enamelled door. Thousands of these stoves were purchased from after WWI. (When I opened my first advertising agency twenty years later, it was in the old Metters building in Elizabeth Street, Sydney.) There were no refrigerators, only ice chests where the ice would be delivered to the house by a bulky man, with the ice block resting on a sugar bag on the top of his shoulder.

Mum had a schedule for cooking the meals. On Monday night we had steak and onions, on Fridays we enjoyed haddock with white sauce, and on Sundays we had a roast meal for lunch. The typical evening meal in most homes was meat and three vegetables. Desserts were custard, jelly, junket or tinned fruit. On special occasions, Dad would take three saucepans to the local Chinese restaurant. One would be filled with chop suey, the other with sweet and sour pork, and the third one with fried rice. Dining at restaurants was rare and takeaway food consisted of fish and chips, usually on Fridays to satisfy Catholic tradition, which was strong in the community. Catholics and Protestants regarded each other with suspicion, and anyone marrying a Catholic had to convert to Catholicism. Several of my aunts did so. The situation is different today, possibly because of the decline in Church attendance and greater acceptance of diverse Faith traditions.

We kept chickens in the large backyard. One chicken would have its head severed for Christmas lunch, and I was horrified to see it running around headless with blood everywhere. The back fence had a choko vine - I would climb up on the roof of the chook house and throw chokos to Robert, my next-door neighbour.

I loved Concord. In the next street was a blacksmith yard owned by two elderly brothers with a few horses. I would collect the manure for our garden. Concord had more parklands than other municipalities in Sydney at the time. At the top of our hill was Concord Golf Club, a private golf club with a bushland area facing the road. Across the golf links was the large Thomas Walker Convalescent Hospital - another place to explore. I would spend hours playing at the golf links with my mates. My best friend was Terry Bissaker, whose father died in WWII. Terry and I were inseparable. His mother, Norma, had a car with a buggy seat in the back. Terry's birthday was in March and to celebrate, his mother took us both to Luna Park. Terry later went into TV production and was talented writing jingles. He claimed to be the writer of the famous *Louie the Fly* commercial for Mortein Fly Spray, although Bryce Courtney also claims this and is popularly believed to be the author. Terry sadly, died in 2001 at sixty years of age.

I attended Mortlake Public School, where my older siblings had attended. Mortlake had a huge gas works and the sound of clanging machinery was constant.

In class, we were separated - boys on one side, girls on the other. We thought girls were from another planet (decades before John Gray's 1992 book *Men Are From Mars, Women Are From Venus*). I avoided talking to girls in fear of being taunted by my mates.

We wrote with wooden pens with a removable steel nib, which were dipped in little white ceramic ink wells sunk into our desks. We lined up to get a fresh supply of ink, making sure we didn't spill it as we carefully returned to our seats. One thing I didn't do was to carve my initials into the desk with the pointed edge of a compass. All learning was by the rote method. We would chant the multiplication table, starting with one and proceeding slowly over the weeks to twelve times twelve. Dad was a great help particularly teaching me the six times table - thanks Dad! Learning history was boring because of all the dates we had to learn, although I enjoyed learning about the early explorers.

All the children were encouraged to drink milk delivered daily to the school. Often the crates were left in the sun. It wasn't too bad in the winter but in summer it was disgusting. I never enjoyed milk again. Also, we were subjected to a series of health check-ups. Hearing, dental, and body co-ordination, along with injections were common.

School games came and went in cycles. A marbles craze gave way to cigarette cards. Cigarettes then came in flat packs with a sleeve holding the cigarettes. We would crush the pack and throw the crushed cards to a wall. The player with the fallen card closest to the wall won. He would throw the other cards against the wall and take the one he wanted. Others would follow, picking the crushed card they liked.

Saturday was the afternoon for the weekly visit to the local Ritz Cinema at the top of Majors Bay Road. My mates and I would arrive early, queue, run down the aisle to sit in the second-front row and push and shove to get to the end seat. Why there? I have no idea.

The Saturday format was virtually the same in all cinemas in Australia. We would all clap and cheer when the lights dimmed, and the huge red curtain opened. We stood (as proud members of the Empire) as *God Save the King* was screened. Then the three serials - twelve to fifteen episodes made cheaply and badly by the main American studio, Republic. All serials ended with a cliff-hanger in which the hero and heroine found themselves in a perilous situation with little apparent chance of escape. Who were they kidding? We all knew they would escape and would appear again next week. The serials were followed by three cartoons. My particular favourites were *Tom and Jerry*, *Mighty Mouse*, and *Heckle and Jeckle*. At interval, we would burst open the doors and run down the street to the milk bar, to buy a packet of Smiths Chips and a bag of lollies. After interval the main film was screened, usually a Western. Afterwards, I would drop into Dad's billiard room via a non-signed door to collect sixpence from Dad then meet up with my mates at Concord Golf Club's bushland to play Cowboys and Indians, hiding and pretending to shoot out among the trees. We would return home when darkness fell.

When I was eight, I cut out film advertisements from the evening papers and stuck them on a board which I hung over the kitchen door. It showed an early interest in either films or advertising—or both! It's not surprising that I went into advertising later on.

A HAPPY CHILDHOOD

I wasn't a great reader as a child. I enjoyed the Biggles series by Captain W. E. Johns, although his books were pro Britain, class ridden and racist - *Biggles in Australia*, portrayed Aboriginal people as subhuman savages. However, I had a hunger for knowledge and I saved my pocket money to buy a second-hand set of encyclopaedias, printed in 1949. Today, I'm not a heavy reader of fiction, preferring nonfiction, biographies, historical, self-help and theological books.

I loved comics. Every Thursday, new ones would appear at the local paper shop. With pocket money, I would buy my favourite comics and store them under my bed in the bedroom that I shared with my brother Bruce. One favourite was *The Phantom*, which is still published today. I mailed a postal note to buy the genuine Phantom skull, which could be bent to place on a finger. My other favourites were *Captain Marvel*, *Archie*, and *Davy Crockett - king of the wild frontier*, based on the life of the American folk hero who died at the Alamo in 1836. In 1954, the Davy Crockett coon cap with a fur tail swept Australia. Thousands of young boys bought one, including me. At school almost every boy wore one!

We would spend annual holidays at Saratoga on the Central Coast, travelling over two hours via bus and train to get there. All the houses we rented had waterfront views of Brisbane Waters. Dad was a keen fisherman and always caught a few fish from our rented boat, while I helped with the rowing. The only thing I hated about Saratoga was the toilet. Before sanitation, the toilet ('dunny') was outside the house and there were a few hurdles to face before using it. First, you had to fight your way through the overgrown bushes. Second on opening the door, you placed a handkerchief drenched in perfume over your nose to reduce the dreaded odour. Then, before sitting on the wooden seat, you had to make sure there were no redback spiders ready to attack. Thank goodness the 'dunny man' would collect the bin every week.

Television arrived in Australia in time for the 1956 Melbourne Olympic Games. To buy a TV set was so expensive that people would bring seats and view it from outside the store window. We eventually bought an Astor black and white set. I remember watching hours of American TV shows - there were a few Australian quiz shows and cooking and music shows, which were all based on their American counter parts. Television started on Channel Nine on 16 September 1956 when Bruce Gyngell said these famous words, 'Good Evening and welcome to television'. This was a great day in Australian history, with Bruce Gyngell followed by two more 'B's - Bob (Dyer) and Bert (Newton). We would quickly eat our evening meal, and then move to the lounge for a night of TV. Sadly, TV finished at 11.30pm, but always with the Christian Epilogue program.

I had an interest in films from a young age, and every Christmas I was given a film book, which would list and illustrate the movies released in that year. During the early 1940s, at the height of Hollywood's Golden Age, studios would distribute photos of their stars. Bruce's favourite was Ingrid Bergman and Dorothy's actor was Alan Ladd. Not to be left out, my pick was Cornel Wilde, one of the most popular stars in the '40s, with an Oscar nomination as Best Actor for his performance in *A Song to Remember* in 1945, based on the life of Frédéric Chopin.

A HAPPY CHILDHOOD

I have happy memories from Mortlake Public School. We used to walk in the hot summer sun for a swim at Cabarita Pool, with cicadas - the popular green grocer, yellow Monday, cherry nose and black prince, the favourite - making a deafening sound. None of us wore a hat. The Queen's visit at Concord Park in 1954 was a big event. 30,000 school children waved our flags madly while the Queen and Prince Philip, standing up in the back of an open Land Rover, waved back.

I played Rugby League at school. I was on the wing and Dad would come and watch me play. I wasn't keen on sports, but I enjoyed running. This lack of interest in sport has stayed with me all of my life.

Terry and I joined the Concord Cub Pack. We dressed in shorts and a shirt, with a scarf around our necks, rolled in a triangle and held together by a 'woggle'. The woollen peaked cap completed the uniform. A wolf's head was sewn on when you completed the Tenderfoot badge. Our leader was Akela, a wolf named after the character in Rudyard Kipling's *Jungle Book*. At the start of the activities, we would sit in a circle before her, squatting on our haunches. 'Dyb, dyb, dyb!' she would cry; the acronym for Do Your Best. 'A-Ke-La! Dob, dob, dob!' we would shout back. Then we would jump up, uttering a frightening wolf cub howl. We could earn badges for things like tying knots, lighting fires, boiling eggs and generally being a good boy. Mum would sew the badges on my sleeve. I advanced to be a leader of one of the four groups, called a Sixer, with duties to lead the Red Six group. I got to wear two yellow stripes on my badge sleeve. After Cubs, Terry and I would walk to busy Parramatta Road for a hamburger and to catch the bus home.

I was also a paper boy. After school, I would collect my strap, purse, newspapers and magazines, and walk up one side and down the other side of Majors Bay Road to the shops and then to Concord Golf Club. I didn't always wear shoes. Once, a piece of matchstick lodged in my heel, requiring the local doctor, Dr Mac, to remove it.

I must have been an honest lad because one time during my paper round, at the regular Wednesday bookmaker's day, I picked up a wad of pound notes from the floor in the bar and handed it in to a surprised barman. Walking back down the long drive from the club to the newsagent, a car pulled up and the driver asked me to return to the club. When we had arrived there, he asked for silence from the noisy bookmakers and said, 'We have an honest boy here. He found a bundle of notes and handed it in. Let's reward Tom for his honesty.' The men gave generously as I was paraded as a hero in the bar. I glowed in the recognition and the thought - it pays to be honest. Days later, Jim McDougall, a Sydney columnist at *The Mirror* newspaper, heard the story and wrote about it - I had no idea at that point, that the media would be where I would focus my efforts and see my success in life! Would there be others?

'Remember that failure is an event,
not a person.'
ZIG ZIGLAR

CHAPTER 3

THE TASTE OF FAILURE

There was to be no success for me just yet, however. At age twelve the time had come for a move to a secondary school. This was the time when individual subject test results were also compared with IQ Tests. I did very well at the exams (top five) but didn't do well in the IQ Test. The sad result was that I was dispatched to Croydon Park Junior Technical School, where Bruce had attended.

It was a complete disaster. I had no interest or ability in technical subjects, woodcraft, metal work or technical drawing. Today, parents would question their child's fit with the school - but not then. Most fellow students became tradesmen.

At a school re-union, years later, there were only two businessmen. The other exception was Steve Woods who, with his father, started Liquorland. They sold it for millions of dollars to Coles, years later.

The male teachers, many returned from the war, were not very good. Only one, my English teacher, Mr Renshaw, took an interest in me. I also joined the wrong crowd of boys who caused me to misbehave, resulting in a frequent punishment of six strokes of the cane on the hand. I was bullied as well, which also upset me. We know the teenage years are a struggle. Sadly I couldn't tell anyone including Mum and Dad about how I felt and what was going on in my life.

I became so depressed and anxious that I cheated in the final exam of the Intermediate Certificate, and was disqualified. This was hard on me and the family. However, I'm proof that there is life after a failed examination. I picked myself up.

Many young people lose their motivation and their self-esteem when they encounter a failure. But failure can spur you on to greater things. It can depend on your attitude to life's struggles. I wanted to succeed. I was so motivated after this negative setback - I made a decision that nothing would get in my way.

School life was not the only problem. My idyllic life at Concord came to an end when an Italian immigrant bought the house we were renting, and we moved to his home in Corunna Road, Petersham. After WWII many immigrants, including Italians, moved into Leichardt and Petersham. They brought with them espresso coffee, pasta and pizzas. They were disparagingly called 'dagoes'. Dad was angry that a 'New Australian' was able to evict us from our idyllic home at Concord.

This was the worst year of my life. At thirteen I was in the wrong school, being bullied, living in a small cramped house in the back room, which slanted down, with a backyard toilet, and dealing with sex and puberty. I felt lonely, too. My friends from Concord went to other, better schools and the few that came with me to Croydon Park still lived at Concord. As the other boys left together after school, I would catch two buses home, alone. I spent my time at the local cinemas, the Strand (I could see the large neon lights from my bedroom) and the Olympia in Parramatta Road, Petersham. I caught buses to see films in nearby Ashfield and Stanmore. The standard programme was a B-grade film followed after the interval with the main feature. Being before television, news reels were popular. Cinesound and Movietone dominated with weekly editions screened. Advertising on the big screen was limited to slides and a voice over commentary.

I became a paper boy again, doing the run every weekday from Parramatta Road to Nelson Street, to a nearby factory, and then positioning myself at the Annandale Pub. The Child Welfare Department was concerned about children selling papers at hotels. One officer, in a gabardine raincoat and carrying a satchel, kept calling on me to move across the road. On his departure, I would quickly pack the papers and magazines and hurry back to the hotel.

The hotel's closing time was six pm, leading to the 'six o'clock swill'. The six pm closing time had started in 1916 as a war time austerity practice and as a response to the Temperance Movement. The six o'clock swill was a last-minute rush to buy drinks before the hotel closed. This became a social problem not helped by the distinctly Australian habit of the 'shout'. This is where, say, one man in a group of five would 'shout' or buy drinks, usually beer, for the other four. Others felt compelled to do the same. With at least five beers, many men went home highly intoxicated.

On Sundays, after watching the wrestling on Saturday nights on my own at nearby Leichardt Stadium, I would get up at five am, have a quick breakfast, collect the papers and push a wheelbarrow around Annandale to sell them. I hate to think what the neighbours thought about my continued early morning whistle-blowing!

Despite, three years at a school I hated, living in a house that was cramped and cold, failing to pass the Intermediate Certificate, and with no desire or encouragement from Mum and Dad to sit for the Leaving School Certificate, or to go to University - I had to motivate myself to 'pull up my socks' and be successful.

Going to University in the 1950s was rare. You had to be ambitious, score high marks with the Leaving Certificate and often aspire to be a doctor or a lawyer. Or, alternatively, you could join another profession. Advertising wasn't a profession at the time, but this was the path I chose.

My early life was marked by two major events. First, leaving Concord for Petersham in 1953, and starting school at Croydon Park. Second, moving from Petersham to Dulwich Hill, to start work in advertising in 1957.

So, after twelve years at Concord and three years at Petersham, I moved to Dulwich Hill on New Canterbury Road, opposite St Paul of the Cross Catholic Church. I started work the same week. After a few of the hardest years of my life, surely things had to get better?'

Things had to get better and they did.

'Build a dream and the dream will build you.'
ROBERT H. SCHULLER

CHAPTER 4

ADVERTISING HERE I COME

The start in advertising didn't come straight away. On leaving school and depressed by not getting my Intermediate Certificate, my Aunt Bessie Glynn found a job for me selling clothes in the Boys' department at Walton's Department Store in Sydney, for six weeks during the Christmas period. I loved it! I was helped by a mentor at Walton's - my boss, who taught me some of the basics of retailing.

After the Christmas period I had to look for another job. In the 1950s there were plenty to choose from. Jobs were advertised in Saturday's *Sydney Morning Herald,* and one stood out to me - a junior at a small advertising agency called R. S. Maynard. My sister accompanied me for the interview with Mr George Webb and, thankfully, he didn't ask for my educational qualifications.

I was successful! I bought a suit, a white shirt and a tie, and started in January 1957. My advertising career was about to take off! This was such a wonderful occasion for me. At last, I was on my way.

R. S. Maynard was one of the oldest agencies in Australia. The founder, Ralph Maynard, had died in 1952. When I joined in 1957 his son John was in charge. John was a short, podgy man, always dressed in a smart grey suit with a waistcoat, who would walk around the small office, sucking on his HB pencil. Like many sons of a successful father, he was not as astute and John knew very little about advertising. Being bored in his large office, doing very little before lunch, he would disappear, saying he was going to see the agency's largest client, the Commercial Banking Company of Sydney (CBC), (now the National Australia Bank) and sometimes he would return later in the afternoon.

Australian advertising agencies in the 1950s were operating in a small market at the outer reaches of the British Empire. After the enforced austerity of the Depression and the war years, Australians were finally able to buy goods, and the advertising industry was ready to help. At that time advertising agencies were not the only companies creating advertisements. Department stores such as Anthony Hordern & Sons, Grace Bros and David Jones had their own departments, and in some cases these were larger than advertising agencies in creative output.

The agencies themselves were still a cottage industry; aside from J. Walter Thompson and Lintas (started by Unilever), the basic Australian agency was a relatively small operation. Most were single city firms and had the name of the entrepreneurial founder who had often started the agency as an account executive or copywriter.

I was put to work with Maynard's senior executive, George Webb, a tall Englishman with a moustache. He handled the major clients: CBC, Lloyd Triestino Shipping Line and Grazcos Co-operative Ltd.

ADVERTISING HERE I COME

The two other male executives were Harvey Looby and George Bishop, who both ran mail order businesses on the side, unknown to Webb and Maynard. Harvey and his father ran a mail order business selling sexy lingerie. They would advertise in a weekly tabloid magazine, called *Weekend*, which was one of my best sellers when I was a paperboy in my youth. Harvey copied a US product, Clearasil, for teenage pimples. He copied the formula and called it 'Teen Aid'. At that stage, the teenage market was booming. I was featured in one of the advertisements - a before photo with pimples (retouched in) and after photo, smiling. I was very excited about this, as not too many young people had such an experience.

George Bishop was the agency accountant. His range of mail order businesses included bust creams, exercise machines and other dodgy products that would likely be banned today. John Maynard and George Webb had no idea that these side businesses were happening.

I don't think John Maynard liked me. He said I didn't have a future in advertising. But I got on well with Harvey (who joined Tom Glynn Advertising years later), George Bishop, a freelance artist, the receptionist, and Judy, the 'tear sheet' lady, who worked in the checking department in a small office on the first floor. Advertisers required that 'tear sheets' (copies of their advert) should accompany the agency's invoice. Postmen would deliver bags of newspapers and magazines with client ads every day. On opening the door Judy, dressed in a grey uniform, would be almost hidden behind the stacks of newspapers and magazines.

We had a lot of fun. The agency interior was very plain. The reception area was a simple counter in front of a plain pegboard.

We decided to paint the office one weekend to improve the image, and make it a bit more colourful - well, it was an advertising agency, a creative business! We misbehaved at times, too. Once Harvey and I were throwing a Perkins Paste bottle back and forth. When Harvey threw it to me, it missed, hit my shoe and flew out of the window to below. I rushed to the window to see if we had killed anyone. Luckily it didn't hit any pedestrians.

'Nothing great was ever achieved without enthusiasm.'
RALPH WALDO EMERSON

CHAPTER 5

MY FIRST BUSINESS

Later, Harvey Looby and George Bishop, now my mentors, helped me establish a mail order business, 'John Power School of Self Confidence'. We selected the face of a handsome man from a photo library to be John Power. Incidentally we almost chose a US Senator, J. F. Kennedy!

We pinched a publication from the US, printed it on foolscap paper and ran small space ads in Sunday newspapers, on an early bottom right position on a right-hand page. Research showed this was the best placement, and it therefore carried a loading (more cost).

The ads I wrote were short and written to attract readership. They included, 'Are you shy?', 'Do you lack self confidence?', 'Do you stutter?', etc. Needy, desperate people would write to the Dulwich Hill PO Box. I would reply with a letter, hoping they would buy the course. If not, I would post a series of follow up letters, reducing the cost of the course each time. I enjoyed collecting the mail from the post office, comparing which advert brought in the greater number and posting the follow up mailings.

Yet another staff member at Maynard's was running a business on the side. That made three. You wonder if any work was done.

John Caples, a copywriter born in New York in the early 1900s, was a pioneer in applying scientific methods in advertising, especially in mail order and direct response. I bought and devoured his ground-breaking and still famous book, *Making Ads Pay: Timeless Tips For Successful Copywriters*. His most famous advertisement was 'They Laughed When I Sat Down At The Piano, But Not When I Started To Play!'

Caples wrote that there are three steps in creating effective ads:
1. Capture the prospect's attention
2. Maintain the prospect's attention
3. Move the prospect to favourable action

In 1960, the credit squeeze hit. Response from the ads dried up. The newspapers increased their advertising rates and I was forced to close the John Power School of Self Confidence. However, I had learned a lot about mail-order advertising and running a small business, and Caples' techniques would be adapted twenty years later when I was writing Charity appeal letters for donation. Nothing in life is wasted.

I also created a product that I thought would sell well, called a Santa Sack. It was a cotton pillowcase with Santa's face on it, which parents would fill with presents. One of Sydney's top illustrators drew the face of a smiling and colourful Santa. I called on Woolworths and Coles, armed with the sample and business proposal, including costings. They didn't buy the concept. Years later, the Chinese produced thousands of them.

MY FIRST BUSINESS

I was employed as a messenger boy, which was how many young men started their careers. There were no messenger girls in those days. In bigger agencies boys would work in the despatch department. Again, there were no girls. My job was delivering advertising materials to the media offices around Hunter Street, hopping on and off buses. When I wasn't running messages and delivering materials, I would mark-up copy for typesetting. I also wrote and designed advertisements for smaller clients like Port Jackson Ferries, which cruised to and from Broken Bay on Sundays. I enjoyed the stimulation of advertising with new things happening every day.

In the late 1950s there were no university or college courses teaching advertising, but there was the School of Applied Advertising, run by a husband and wife team, Mr and Mrs Hall. Both were elderly and had the market to themselves. Helen Hall was a stern headmistress type with no sense of humour. When I arrived late for my first interview with her to be accepted in her famed School, I was reprimanded for being late. Never again! Tucked away in a tiny, pokey office in Willmot Street, we would sit in rows on uncomfortable chairs for the lectures. We would receive a booklet after the weekly lecture with a list of things to do for homework. My brother Bruce also did the course when he returned from London and Toronto, before following me into advertising agencies.

Maynard's was a sleepy ad agency. The clients were loyal, and during my time there, there were no new clients. Although television had come to Australia, the company had no television clients. They also lost the AMP business leaving CBC as their largest client. George Webb would create the ads, which were booked in metropolitan and country towns where the CBC had a branch. Most newspapers were printed by letterpress machines, which required a type of printing plate call a 'stereo'. Every month I would wrap the stereos with newspaper, insert the booking slip, tie with string, and carry them to the post office.

Having learnt the basics of advertising, selecting media, marking up copy for typesetting, doing layouts and running a small mail order business, it was time to move up and meet the man who would change my life.

'Whatever the mind can conceive
and believe, it can achieve.'
NAPOLEON HILL

CHAPTER 6

RISING

After three years at Maynard's, it was time to move, and again an advertisement in Saturday's *Sydney Morning Herald* prompted me to apply for an Assistant Account Executive position at Jackson Wain - a relatively new and fast growing, highly successful agency located at North Sydney.

It's interesting to look back on your life and see the strategic events that made you the person you are today. Meeting Frank Grace and joining Jackson Wain was one of these events.

Peter James, a Pom who had served in the Royal Navy, ran the advert. He interviewed me in their office in North Sydney, and I was given the job. Peter handled the contracts for Formica, Rexall drugs and Rembrandt cigarettes, which was a new brand from Rothmans, one of their largest clients. His main client was Formica surfaces, a competitor to Laminex. He asked me to do a research study about Formica, their distributors, architects, kitchen manufacturers and consumers. This was an important strategy to understand the many target groups in their advertising. I liked Peter, who remained a good friend and mentor for many years after I left the agency.

The founder, John Jackson, was a large, pleasant, rotund man who also ran a pharmaceutical company. I found out later he was interested in the Christadelphians, a small Christian denomination. Mid Wain, his partner, was a quiet man who enjoyed betting on horses. They were not really involved in servicing clients, they were mainly figureheads. The client work was left to the Directors, who distributed the work amongst the staff. The driving force was Frank Edward Grace, a short, fat accountant who joined the agency in the 1950s. This man had a tremendous impact on me.

I first met Frank at a presentation with Peter James to gain the business of a potential client, conservative Tasmanian jam maker IXL. Up until then I hadn't met Frank. Peter James, Frank Grace and I were in IXL's impressive wood panelled boardroom in Newtown. Grace started the presentation with these words, 'There's a number of ways you can f____ a woman. So it is with advertising - there are many ways to advertise!'

That was certainly a jolt to my system. I wasn't expecting that!

His statement not only shocked me, but I had no idea what effect this would have on the client. Frank Grace also had no idea who the client was. Were they conservative? Did they appreciate his coarse language from someone wanting to work with them? I think the conservative client was shocked, too. Grace asked me to phone the agency for some information regarding a media question, which I did.

IXL was an iconic Australian brand name said to have been created from the founder's personal motto, 'I excel in everything I do'. Despite Grace's opening comment, Jackson Wain landed the account. The next day I was transferred to Frank Grace's group. I obviously impressed him. I don't know how Peter James took this. He had interviewed and employed me as his assistant and was impressed by my work. He liked me, and a Director had poached me.

I should point out that I have always looked for mentors - perhaps a father figure, as Dad lacked some qualities to have a strong influence on me. At Maynard's, George Webb and Harvey Looby had been great mentors, encouraging me to start a small business. At Jackson Wain, FEG (as Frank Grace was known), influenced me so much that I still dream about him. What did I like about him? Despite being crude and cruel with staff, I admired his ability and success in handling a range of highly profitable clients, including well-known products such as Sunbeam, Simpson Washing Machines and Supertex fabrics. He also headed up the agency's grocery brands: White Wings, Cobbity Farm Bakeries, the NSW Rice Board, the Tea Council and the Australian Dairy Produce Board, promoting butter and cheese. FEG had four young men in their early twenties as his assistants. Women in those days were mainly employed as secretaries, or in studio production and administration, although there were two women copywriters at Jackson Wain.

The four of us had small offices outside FEG's office. After lunch, normally downstairs in the agency kitchen, he would briskly walk down the corridor and shout the name of who he wanted to see. We would go into his office and receive our instructions.

After finishing as Peter James' assistant, my new senior account manager and boss became Peter Maegraith, a tall likeable man - the only child of Kerwin Maegraith, a famous cartoonist of the

'30s and '40s. Peter had come from another large agency where he was a layout artist, and he now handled some large accounts at Jackson Wain.

FEG had created a unique way to boost income by combining the Australian Dairy Produce Board with other food clients, and later the Bake-Off with the Dairy Board and White Wings. By doing this Jackson Wain received billings from non-JW clients. This was a clever strategy.

Peter Maegraith was terrified of two bullies - one was FEG and the other a demanding man from the Dairy Board in Melbourne. This made communication difficult with daily phone calls. Sadly, Peter eventually fell out with FEG. He suffered the usual practice when a person 'fell from Grace', words that I used to describe the many people who would leave the agency. They were placed in a downstairs office until they found another job - a soul-destroying experience. It upset me as I was fond of Peter.

I had a great four years at Jackson Wain. I was a favourite son, was eager and keen to impress and I created some unique campaigns. It was unusual for a 'suit' - an account executive - to create campaigns.

For White Wings, I created a tie-in promotion with a Walt Disney 1962 film, *Search of the Castaways*, starring teenage actor Hayley Mills and popular French actor Maurice Chevalier. It featured New Zealand and was a perfect tie-in. The contest prize was a trip to New Zealand. In creating the tie-in, I received free air travel to and from New Zealand, where I took a holiday and hitchhiked over the two islands.

White Wings advertised heavily on TV and the company was a part sponsor of Bobby Limb's *Sound of Music*, a top rating programme on Channel 9 from 1963 to 1972. I was supervising a live TV studio commercial for one of White Wings puddings. It was shot in a few hours, whereas a commercial filmed in a TV production studio or on location may take many more hours, up to a day. A two or three second shot could take up to half a day to shoot. At Channel 9, to film the dessert, we substituted shaving cream for real cream. After the commercial was completed, a technician scooped up the shaving cream in his fingers and ate it - and quickly spat it out!

I also created and implemented a project with Cobbity Farm Bakery, which was part of White Wings. Cobbity Farm was expanding its bread home delivery service, and this was a test market. A leaflet would be inserted in the letterbox, advising a Cobbity Farm baker would be calling with a free breadbasket if they signed up for home delivery. In the early sixties, women were generally at home - very few worked. The test market suburb was Engadine, an outlying area of Sydney. In my holidays, I walked the streets delivering leaflets into letterboxes. The next day I returned, making calls and signing up customers. At one house, an attractive young woman in a brief bikini offered me a coffee. Wow - that was not what I had expected, so I fled!

I also worked on Akubra hats and would wear one to see the clients, with whistles from the young women. I quite liked that attention. The young women were mainly secretaries. One was Gay Porter, the daughter of pioneer animator, Eric Porter who had learnt his craft by the influence of Walt Disney. Eric started Eric Porter Studios and it is said he was the inspiration for the character of Mr Sheen, a cleaning product. Gay later changed her name to Gaby. Sixty years on, Gaby and her husband John are our neighbours at Pearl Beach, and Gaby is a famous sculptor. Another secretary was Val Osborne who married, Colin, who was an account director on the Rice Board. She is also one of our neighbours. It's a small world.

The agency encouraged the staff to buy the clients' products and services. I did buy them when working and I often still buy them today.

I have always been ambitious. A talented copywriter from England advised me to be patient and to learn as much as I could, and time would do the rest. I was a man in a hurry, and I found it difficult to be patient, but this was good advice and I valued what this man had said.

Some interesting people passed through the agency. One was Donald Horn, author of *The Lucky Country*. I think he was employed as a celebrity to project the intellectual image of the agency. He wrote several editorial style adverts for Qantas, and worked on the launch of Rupert Murdoch's new national newspaper, *The Australian*. Another celebrity was Leo Schofield, a creative director who went on to start his own agency with two others and later became a food writer. He used to fight with the manager of the TV department. Leo used to say that their main role was to make it difficult to produce commercials!

Freelance people, such as photographers, artists, and TV studios, made stacks of money working with Jackson Wain. Many talented freelance artists staffed the agency. Most were outstanding artists who would render the ads or TV storyboards in colour, before today's practice of a copywriter and artist working together. The computer radically changed the graphic art industry. Artists before were trained at Art School and all could draw. Now with the right computer program almost anyone can draw.

Working in an advertising agency was a fun experience despite the deadlines, creative submissions, and putting up with huge egos. I worked long hours producing joint promotions for the food clients, but I loved it.

My friend, a typographer in the production department, typed a memo to me, ostensibly from Frank Grace, saying that, because I was so good at producing artwork, I was being transferred to the production department. I was furious. I stormed into Grace's office and demanded to know what was going on. He read the memo and saw that it was a joke and made some sarcastic comment about my ability. He asked me to find the culprit and tell him, but I didn't bother. I guess I was too busy and pleased to stay where I was to be concerned about this incident. Just another day at the office!

The agency produced a stage show performed, at a nearby Church hall. I appeared twice. Once in a walk-on role as an enthusiastic account executive, striding quickly across the stage. The other appearance was in a send up of TV Westerns. They were my first claims to fame! - and, the only times I have appeared acting on a stage.

The agency believed in the value of training their employees. They paid for my tuition at the School of Applied Advertising and would organise lunches with a visiting speaker. Meat pies would be served for lunch, which was okay with me. The good workers in the company were offered shares. I bought a few hundred shares - this was my first investment in stocks and shares, and I felt very important having launched out into the big wide world of finance. Things were going well, I was having fun, and my career was on its way. I had no idea that another big change was about to hit, nor that it would involve someone you didn't expect to find in the advertising world – God.

'God comes disguised as your life.'
PAULA D'ARCY

CHAPTER 7

GOD AND GLYNN

Like most children of the 1940s and '50s, I attended Sunday School. Parents were keen to have their children receive moral training, and at the same time often allowing the parents to sleep in.

Church going was strong in Australia at the time, being predominantly the Catholics, the Anglicans and the Protestants. My family were Presbyterians from Scottish stock. I was christened at St David's Presbyterian Church at Haberfield. Many Baby Boomers attended Sunday school. I did the rounds of Sunday Schools in Concord, but never stayed long at any of them. After attending Sunday School at St Mary's Anglican Church, a lovely elderly lady gave me a card with Psalm 23. She encouraged me to become a Christian. Most pictures in Church halls had a painting of a feminine looking Jesus in a white garment, holding a lamb. I didn't have any other religious training, although Mum and Dad would encourage me to recite the Lord's Prayer at bedtime.

When we moved to Dulwich Hill in 1957, the three unhappy years at Petersham and Croydon Park Technical School had to come to an end. I had started work but had no friends. I saw an advertisement in the local *Western Suburbs Courier* advertising the Boys' Brigade at Dulwich Hill Baptist Church (ads in newspapers played a big part in my life). I walked into the hall and, unlike an earlier, unsuccessful encounter with the Boys' Brigade at Stanmore Baptist Church, where I had found the boys to be too old, here I not only met boys of my age, but some wonderful adults as well. Possibly this was replacing my home life where Dad was gambling heavily and Mum was not happy with his lack of being a good provider. My home wasn't a happy home, and I felt embarrassed to invite people there. Soon I was attending Sunday School in the morning, then morning Church, followed by Christian Endeavour in the afternoon, and then evening Church and supper.

Christian Endeavour was a youth movement in many Protestant Churches. It involved young people leading a meeting, speaking to a paper they wrote, reading the Bible in public and praying. It was a wonderful way for teenagers to build confidence and knowledge of the Bible. Later, politician Fred Nile became National Director of the Australian Christian Endeavour movement from 1964 to 1967. Then in 2006, despite CE struggling, Fred organised the National Christian Endeavour Convention. It is sad now to see CE decline.

Youth camps were popular. The Baptist Church had three camps in bushland around Sydney. Over a weekend, from Friday night to Sunday afternoon, hundreds of teenagers from Baptist Churches would attend to hear a minister talk about their Faith, with the emphasis on being converted. On Saturday nights we would sit around a blazing campfire, singing hymns before being sent off to bed. Then the fun started. Some of the boys would raid the girls' cabins. But the leaders knew what was going on, turning up and telling us to go back to our beds.

One year, on one of the hottest days in January at a camp at Macquarie Fields, I went for a swim to cool down on a Sunday. The leaders found out and I was sent home for disobeying their instructions. This was an early example of becoming a rebel. It has continued as I have often fought against silly rules and regulations since! Years later, I met a woman who was also at the camp, who was shocked by the penalty.

Memories of blazing campfires, reminds me of Empire Day celebrations on 24 May each year, which ended with a bonfire and fireworks called 'crackers'. Many open areas (and there were a lot in the 1940s around Sydney) had a huge bonfire, with a Guy Fawkes character at the top. For weeks prior I would buy fireworks from the local paper shop and store them in a drawer, bringing them out periodically to examine them. I preferred the deafening loud double bungers, tom thumbs and throw downs, rather than the prettier roman candles and rockets.

At the Dulwich Hill Baptist Church Boys' Brigade Company, the captain was Ken Jarvis, who worked with NSW Child Welfare. He was the son of Rev Wilfrid Jarvis, an outstanding minister, who spent a record time at Stanmore Baptist Church. Ken later became CEO of Mission Australia. Like the Cubs and Scouts we had our special uniform: blue, with a peaked cap, pants, shirt and a belt. The programme was basic. Drill marching up and down the hall followed by a Bible story. Then we would change into a singlet, shorts and sandshoes, for games and jumping over the dreaded wooden horse! I met some good friends. On Saturday mornings we would gather on the corner of New Canterbury and Marrickville Roads, outside the shopping centre, to watch the passing parade, mainly girls. In the afternoon, we would ride our bikes to Maroubra Beach, returning home sunburnt many hours later.

On Sunday night after Church, we would walk to the bottom of my street and talk for a long time. On the New Year's Eve of 1960 we celebrated the start of the '60s, I coined the new decade as the 'Sexy Sixties' - and I was right. The contraceptive pill arrived in Australia in 1961 - we were the second country in the world to receive it. But the pill had no effect on the teenagers at Dulwich Hill Baptist Church. The sexual revolution passed us by. Sex outside marriage was rare, although kissing and petting were common. Some friends, frustrated by restrictions on sexual activity, married very young, in their late teens or early twenties. The minister would give them advice on what makes a good Christian marriage, but sadly, many marriages still failed.

Another mentor was the minister, Albert Dube, a kind, gentle man who had pioneered missionary work in Papua New Guinea. The Baptists have always been active and strong in overseas missionary work. After WWII, Baptist chaplains who had returned from Papua New Guinea had seen the vision of establishing a mission in the Highlands, working in education and health. In 1948 the NSW and ACT Baptist Churches agreed with this vision and started missionary work there. Albert had returned from New Guinea with artefacts, which he proudly showed off during his sermon. One that took our attention was a 'gourd' traditionally worn by Highland males to cover their genitals. They looked big. I wondered what the naïve young teenage girls thought.

Another mentor was Ken MacArthur, the owner of a successful confectionary wholesale company, who was my Sunday School teacher.

In the '50s and '60s Baptists were seen by some people as a small fundamental denomination. The media depicted Baptists as dogmatic, 'Bible-bashing' religious bigots; narrow and straight-laced wowsers, who were opposed to the main traditional pleasure of the typical Australian male: beer, gambling, and sex. Although 'wowser' has long been a somewhat derogatory term in Australia, usually meaning a teetotalling prude, Baptists happily accepted the term, deciding it stood for 'We Only Want Social Evils Removed'.

The Baptist Church was evangelical, focused on saving people from hell, or separation from God. Yet the folk were friendly and lived good, simple lives. It gave young people boundaries and kept them from alcohol, smoking, gambling and drugs. Frequently, they would hold an evangelical week of meetings where people outside the Church would be invited and prayerfully urged to make a 'decision for Christ'. A New Zealand minister's visit put pressure on me to give my life to Christ. I wasn't ready - yet! But God had something up his sleeve.

Jesus: 'If you hold to my teaching, you are really my disciples. Then you will know the truth, and the truth will set you free.'

JOHN 8:31 NIV

CHAPTER 8

CONVERTED

It started with an argument with Mum over arranging a possible twenty-first birthday party. This caused a split in our relationship. I was angry at the family for not hosting a party, so I spent my twenty-first birthday with a few friends at Kings Cross instead.

My relationship with girls was another factor. I dated Church going girls and attended youth camps and the monthly Baptist Youth Fellowship meetings at the Central Baptist Church in George Street. I became the publicity person for BYF. I also dated non-Church going girls. However a young woman I liked from Jackson Wain rejected me, causing me to adopt an anti-Church stance.

The minister, Norm Chambers, noticing my absence from Church, caught up with me, sat me down in his study and asked, 'Tom, what do you really want?' - a good question to ask anyone going through a crisis. I said, 'Like every young person - fame, fortune and fun'. He replied, 'Marilyn Monroe wanted those things and she died from a drug overdose in 1962'. That hit me hard, a standoff with the family and a failed romance. I was in a crisis! Do I reject the Faith or embrace it?

I had planned to go camping in my new, red VW Beetle with a good friend from Church, Ken Harrison, but he had declined at the last minute. So, I went by myself with three books: the Bible; *Basic Christianity* by John Stott, a leading Anglican minister at All Souls, Langham Place, London; and a book of sermons by Harry Emerson Fosdick, a liberal Baptist minister at the Riverside Church in uptown New York. The Riverside Church had been built by philanthropist and businessman, John D. Rockefeller, a Baptist.

At this stage, I was drifting away from the black and white view of the Bible. I questioned, did a whale really swallow Jonah? Was the world created 6,000 years ago in one day in October? Were Daniel's friends burnt to death in the fiery furnace? Many Christians believe these stories all actually happened. However I saw them as myths telling vital truths about God's faithfulness to His people.

During this camping time on my own, I had time to reflect, whereupon I finally accepted Jesus, not because of my sins and as a pathway to heaven, but because of His life, ministry, death, and resurrection, and as the One to follow. I was also impressed by Jesus' disciples, who had witnessed His resurrection and who went on to claim that He was the Son of God. They kept the Faith when facing death. I was also impressed by St Paul with his dramatic and life changing conversion on the road to Damascus, and with his letters to small struggling Churches in Asia Minor.

I returned a changed person. Apologised to Mum, was baptised, and threw myself into a new mission - to bring the insights of advertising/marketing into the Church. Like any new convert, I wanted to tell people about the Faith.

In 1959, Australians experienced a religious revival - a result of the well-planned and executed Billy Graham Crusade. The Baptists threw themselves into the Crusade. A media commentator said, 'of all the religious groups who assisted in the Crusade, it was the Baptists who worked the hardest'. The Church hired a bus to take folk to and from the Sydney Cricket Ground. The final meeting on Sunday, 10 May 1959 at the Sydney Showground attracted a world record Crusade crowd of 150,000 people. This Crusade had a huge impact. Theological colleges burst with new students and Churches welcomed new people. Two brothers who were converted at the Crusade went on to have a powerful influence in the Sydney Anglican Diocese. Peter Jensen, Anglican Archbishop of Sydney from 2001 to 2013, was 15 years old when he was converted; and his brother Philip, who later became Dean of St Andrew's Anglican Cathedral, was converted at age 13.

I pestered Mum, Dad and Bruce to attend. They found Billy Graham and the Crusade interesting, but did not respond, despite my prayers.

Another Crusade was the Missouri-Australia Crusade in 1964. Here, 160 ministers from Missouri, USA flew to Australia and visited Australian Churches to conduct crusades. Some 355 Churches participated. The ministers from Missouri were part of the Southern Baptist Convention of USA - the second-largest denomination in the US. The NSW Baptists were greatly influenced by the American denomination, and introduced all age Sunday Schools and Church fundraising strategies. Different to NSW, in Victoria, a more liberal and progressive theology prevailed.

At Dulwich Hill Baptist Church we were host to a likeable Missouri pastor. Surprisingly, the visit to Australia from these genuine Christian pastors was successful, despite the obviously different culture and the practice of race discrimination in the Southern States of America. I raised their treatment of different races with our guest. He truly couldn't see a problem. It would never happen today. These men dedicated to preaching were not all evangelists but usually pastors from small Churches in Missouri. One incidental new habit I learned from the pastors was drinking water with a meal!

A well-known Baptist, Rev Alan Prior, was in charge and, as a young, enthusiastic, new Christian, I visited him and offered to do the promotion. I created the advertising with the artwork produced by friend, Graham Wade of Pilgrim Art Studio. The resulting Hymn book with the logo is still found in Churches today.

> 'Only mad dogs and Englishmen
> go out in the midday sun.'
> NOEL COWARD

CHAPTER 9

SINGAPORE - COLONIAL STYLE

By May 1964, despite my new-found Faith, I had become unsettled and, at age 23, I decided to travel to London, where my brother Bruce had lived in the 1950s. I went into Frank Grace's office and said I was resigning to go to London. 'No, you're not Glynn, you're going to Singapore,' he yelled. 'Singapore? Where's Singapore?' I replied. So, not long after finding Singapore in an atlas, I sailed out of Sydney on a cold afternoon in June 1964, ready for a new adventure, with family and Church friends throwing streamers from the wharf.

In 1964, after the collapse of the Common Market, Australian companies looked to Asia. With two large clients, Qantas and the Australian Dairy Produce Board, Jackson Wain opened an office in Singapore as a springboard from where offices in Hong Kong, Bangkok and Kuala Lumpur, could be established and supervised.

Jackson Wain was the first Australian agency to open an office overseas. I was sent to work under John Shadwell, a talented, creative copywriter. He had worked in Bangkok and now had transferred to Singapore.

We started at Jackson Wain's affiliate agency, Young Advertising, on the corner of Orchard and Scotts Road, Singapore. Three of us shared an office: John, a secretary and me. With only two clients, Qantas, and the Australian Dairy Produce Board, we knew we had to grow. ADPB and Malaysian Dairy Industries had become a joint venture in 1963, producing cans of condensed milk - the main one was 'Baby Stork' which required pack designs and promotion. The company was one of the first at Jurong, an industrial estate built on reclaimed land. The opening of their factory was a big event, with politicians and business people from Australia and Singapore in attendance.

We soon had other large clients, including Proctor and Gamble, Horlicks and Fitzpatrick's Supermarket. The agency moved to a recently built Chinese Chamber of Commerce Building in Hill Street, opposite the American Embassy. It's still there, despite the huge number of buildings surrounding it.

When I had first arrived in Singapore, I stayed a few nights at the (then tiny) old Orchard Hotel in Orchard Road, before moving into an out-building in a large colonial-built house with large gardens. This was filled with such lovely colours in the flora and fauna - it was rather amazing to see. An elderly English-born woman, Miss Bach, ran the home with the help of her adopted Chinese son. During WWII the Japanese had used the home as a brothel. Sadly, the building is no longer standing.

I threw myself into the work. John Shadwell worked on getting new business and I served the current clients. We were a

SINGAPORE - COLONIAL STYLE

good team, and that's important when working on campaigns. It also made work life more enjoyable!

In the second year the agency really took off, which was great for all of us. It was so exciting to see new business continually coming into our agency. In October 1965 we were excited and thrilled with the appointment of Malaysian Singapore Airlines (later Singapore Airlines and Malaysian Airlines). It was one of the largest accounts in South East Asia. I handled the account in nine markets - Singapore, Malaysia, Hong Kong, Thailand, Japan, the Philippines, the US, the UK and Australia. It was a big responsibility, but I thrived on the busyness these accounts gave me.

Why was Jackson Wain, Singapore so successful? Most Singapore agencies were quite mediocre at that time. The largest one, and our competitor, was Cathay Advertising, started in 1946 by Australian Elma Kelly. Cathay was the first overseas agency opened since the War. The answer to our success was largely that John Shadwell was an outstanding creative ad-man, he was eminently professional, and he was brilliant at writing copy and creating campaigns. Always chewing a cigarette, John had incredibly high energy and walked and talked very quickly, while he chewed away. Unfortunately, he also drank too much. In some ways this was to his disadvantage, but on the other hand, to his credit he came up with wonderful ad campaigns. Some exceptional art directors from the Sydney office would stop over for a few days when they were on their way to London, to help with the creative work, and to attract new clients. This also helped us tremendously.

John was joined later by Peter Beaumont, a Jackson Wain client in Sydney before coming to Singapore. There was no way Shadwell and Beaumont could work together; they just couldn't communicate with each other and they had different ideas. Peter opened the Kuala Lumpur office with the huge Rothmans account and built a successful agency. Joined by his girlfriend, they became connected to Malay business, Government, and royalty. They stayed many years in Kuala Lumpur, and I would visit them when passing through. I think Peter may have converted to Islam, although I can't be sure of this. Malaysia is predominantly Islamic, so it is quite possible.

From the heady days with a start-up staff of only three, it grew to a staff of 33 by the time I left in July 1966, after only two years. This rapid growth was due to being a new agency in Singapore, the energy and talent of John Shadwell in getting new business, and my role as servicing and managing the accounts. I think being an Australian agency helped, also.

I loved Singapore. It was still a colonial city without the big buildings. Of course, it's totally different now, while a very successful country financially and commercially.

The other guests were a mixed lot. It reminded me of a scene from Terence Rattigan's play and film, *Separate Tables*. Most of the guests were English, some being retired. Included in the group was an artist who had been with *The Straits Times* and interned by the Japanese during the War, as well as a retired colonel and his wife. We had our meals there, served by Chinese servants. I stayed at other homes of friends, but I loved to return sometimes as the prodigal son, and was always welcomed warmly by Miss

Bach. She was worried that I may have been influenced by loose living!

Known as the black and white houses, because of their dark timber beams with whitewashed walls, these homes were originally built by British Colonial families. They were double storey, with large verandas and overhanging roofs. The houses were designed with high ceilings, shutter-style windows, and open concept layouts to allow the breeze to pass through. Due to Singapore's rapidly growing population, many of these houses have since been demolished in favour of more space-efficient housing. I loved Singapore. At the time, it was still a colonial city without the big buildings. Of course, it's totally different now, while a very successful country financially and commercially. But even then, we could see that change was coming.

'Oh, East is east, and west is west, and never the twain shall meet.'
RUDYARD KIPLING

CHAPTER 10

SINGAPORE ON THE MOVE

Change was in the air in Singapore. Once British colonies, Singapore, Malaysia and Borneo had gained their independence. The countries became known as Malaysia, but the combined nation didn't last. On 9 August 1966, Lee Kuan Yew, the Singapore Prime Minister, appeared on TV and became very emotional. He broke down, rubbing the tears from his eyes. He said, 'Singapore is on its own. We have severed our ties with Malaysia, and we will build our own future'. This was quite a statement and took everyone by surprise.

Confrontation between Malaysia and Indonesia became very violent. There was a three-year conflict, in the years from 1963 to 1966, before the new federation of Malaysia was stabilised. On 10 March 1965 a bomb exploded at MacDonald House, killing three people and injuring 35 others. This was a very dangerous time. Due to this incident, the Singapore Government introduced a curfew. I had flown to Kuala Lumpur on Qantas business and returned late one night. While walking to my house I heard a car speeding behind me. Thinking it could be a terrorist, I turned around perspiring, dropped my case and put my arms up. I was scared, not knowing what was going to happen to me. But it was the police telling me I had broken the curfew and needed to go home. This was still quite a fearful event as the police could have arrested me.

My family back home was afraid for me after the bombing. I explained it was like living in Sydney and a bomb going off in the CBD - I was living in the suburbs and was a long way away from the City.

Within twenty years, Lee Kuan Yew had transformed Singapore from a tiny island City into one of the best run economic miracles of the twentieth century. He had done an amazing job, but not everyone was happy with him. Even so, he did enjoy wide popularity, running a one-party Republic, with censorship and strong social laws against long hair and chewing gum etc. You can't please everyone!

Most of my spare time (when I had any) I spent driving my black MG Midget car exploring Singapore, with short trips over the causeway into Malaysia. I tried to learn the local Malay language and had a lovely Malay woman as a teacher. Sadly, I was not good at learning languages and instead spent all the time asking about her life, religion (Islam), family, the house she lived in, and how she co-existed with the Chinese, the largest ethnic group in Singapore. This helped me to better understand the culture of the people.

I became a member of the Singapore Swimming Club. Membership was mainly open to expatriates.

Being single, I met many Chinese, Malay, Indian and Eurasian women, and the daughters aged around sixteen to eighteen of English Army officers. They were from boarding schools in the

UK and were on summer holidays - I took a few out on dates, but because of their young ages nothing developed romantically. Anyway, they had to return to their boarding schools in England in the September of that year.

It was great to have the company of women!

One young woman I took out was called Madeleine, an attractive Chinese woman, and another one was Lorna, a Eurasian who worked in the next office. Lorna was a Catholic, with an English father and Indian mother. She had been recently divorced. Sadly, although I enjoyed our relationship, our personalities clashed, and we parted. Lorraine, a girl I knew in Sydney, came to visit but nothing developed between us. Surrounded by all these women but going nowhere!

Not many expatriates married local woman. They were only girlfriends, because there was still a stigma against marrying Asians. Which is a sad thing to admit, but thankfully it's different now.

I had become a Christian in 1962, and I was keen to connect with other Christians. Church life in Singapore was interesting. There were many Christian denominations started by English and Europeans missionaries in the 1800s. Of all the Faiths, about 20% are Christians, according to a survey in 2015. Of those, about 38.5% are Catholics and 61.5% mainly Protestants. The Anglican St Andrew's Cathedral was established in 1856. It is an impressive building, located on prime real estate facing the sea. The Armenian Church is the oldest Church in Singapore, established in 1835.

On the first Sunday after my arrival, I took a taxi to an English-speaking Baptist Church in the suburbs. The Church was sponsored by the Southern Baptist Convention of the USA. At the evening service the minister concluded with an altar call, which encouraged people to go forward and accept Jesus as their Lord. I was not used to this approach - it seemed a bit strange to me, so I decided instead I would worship at the Wesley Methodist Church, the oldest Methodist Church in Singapore. I was more comfortable in this Church. The ministers were from the UK, they were good preachers, and the bulk of the Congregation were middle class, university educated Chinese.

Being an expatriate and possibly one of the youngest, I met people I wouldn't have in Sydney. We are generally communal people, preferring to belong to people like us. Up to then in Sydney most of my friends were Christians. In Singapore I enjoyed meeting folk from other countries, who I found were kind and generous. I met such a great variety of people, and I enjoyed this very much - it was so much more interesting.

Below the surface there was a lot of drinking and, sadly, many marriage breakdowns. An English artist explained that back home his wife would stay home with the children. Here she didn't work (wives couldn't get a job) and with too much time to fill, she became involved with another man and divorce followed.

A well-known Christian mission, Overseas Mission Fellowship, had been evicted by the communists from China in the mid 1950s and had moved their headquarters to Singapore in 1964. Previously known as China Inland Mission (CIM), it was founded by J. Hudson Taylor in 1865. It was the forerunner of the Faith Missions movement, where intending missionaries had to fund part or all of their expenses. On Friday nights the Mission ran a prayer meeting, and I would attend, looking to

SINGAPORE ON THE MOVE

meet young, female missionaries. I wanted to meet someone for company. Despite the good things I had to offer, and the fact that as a good Baptist, I didn't smoke or drink, they were obviously committed to their calling! It didn't matter - I knew there would be a wonderful woman for me somewhere.

My time in Singapore brought me many good things, including a wonderful close friendship with May and Harvey Stanley. from England. Harvey was an engineer manager at Rediffusion, the local radio station. They lived in a typical black and white bungalow and were devoted Christian people. It was great having them as my friends - they were a lovely couple. On Sundays I would drive to the Sands Soldiers Home on the UK Army Compound to teach young boys at a Sunday School. The British Army still had a presence there. After teaching the boys I had a delicious lunch, cooked by a delightful Malay couple. I also taught Bible stories at a Singapore Chinese Mission in the Chinatown slums. This all kept me very busy while meeting new people, which I enjoyed.

When lunching in an air-conditioned restaurant, I would smile at the English tourists walking around in the middle of the day, with no hat, and sandals with rolled up socks. The scene reminded me of Noel Coward's ditty, 'Mad dogs and Englishmen go out in the midday sun'. He wrote this while driving from Hanoi to Saigon, in Vietnam. Tourists had to be careful while walking, not to fall into the deep gutters built to take the monsoon rains. Today they are all covered over, which is much safer.

'Going troppo' is an Australian term for people living in the tropics affected by the unrelenting heat and humidity. Singapore is just north of the Equator, with no changes in the seasons apart from the two monsoon periods. The average temperature is about 31 degrees Celsius. I must admit, the heat was gruelling at times. I did miss the four separate seasons in Sydney.

Expatriates working in Singapore normally sign contracts for two years before returning home to enjoy the seasons, particularly winter. I spent two years in Singapore, unlike my son Steve and his wife Gemma with their two children, who later spent nine years there. But they had regular trips home, which pleased me, as I did miss them.

In early 1966 I became burnt out with overwork, the climate, and a complicated relationship with Lorna. I was exhausted and, not knowing it, I was falling into depression.

This was the first time it had struck. I felt tired, I felt low, with little motivation and I thought it was a result of the breakdown in the relationship with Lorna. As an extrovert, I hid it from my work and flatmates. I still appeared bushy tailed and enthusiastic - I didn't want anyone knowing I was depressed. I would have been embarrassed, as at that time there was some stigma about this. Thankfully that is not the case today!

An artist friend from Jackson Wain stayed with me on his way to London and did work on the airline account. He was good company and was getting over a failed relationship. We would share our experiences of love gone wrong. It didn't help me when he sang 'Lorna standing there in her underwear', based on the song *Laura*. I sought help from a doctor for my depression, who prescribed Valium and gave me injections to lift my mood.

In June 1966, after two years of an exciting job, meeting interesting people and experiencing a relationship breakdown, I decided to return to Australia, packed gifts and souvenirs and sold the MG Midget. While work had been exciting and enjoyable, the broken romance with Lorna caused me to feel burnt out. Overall, it had been an up and down period, which somehow I got through - or with grit and determination I got through.

I sailed to Perth, and spent a night at a party with some advertising people. This was the swinging '60s, so anything went. After conservative Singapore this was a culture shock. The following day I caught a plane to Sydney. The next chapter of my life was about to begin.

'In London, everyone is different, and that means anyone can fit in.'
PADDINGTON BEAR

CHAPTER 11

LONDON SWINGS

What next or where next? Back home from Singapore, I received a call from Frank Grace to re-join the agency in Sydney. I reminded him that I had wanted to go to London before he had side-tracked me to Singapore!

Travelling to London was a rite of passage for many young Australians. Bruce was there in the early 1950s. He had to leave because he was called up for National Service. Not wanting to be a soldier (like me, he didn't like bloodshed), he had fled to Ontario, Canada.

In fact, if I had returned to Singapore, to handle the Malaysian Singapore Airlines account again, my life may have turned out differently. MSA was handled by Jackson Wain, Sydney. Ian Batey worked on the Qantas account and when the MSA partnership was terminated in 1972, Batey jumped ship to launch his own agency with the newly independent Singapore Airlines as his foundation client. The Singapore Girl campaign, ('A Great Way to Fly') was a huge world-wide success. Batey Advertising was one of the stars of the South East Asian advertising industry from the '70s to the '90s. So much for what could have been, if I'd returned to Singapore.

Having spent a few weeks in Sydney, and enjoying my first winter in two years, I flew out to London. I spent a long time travelling there, staying a week each in Tahiti, Mexico City, Los Angeles and New York. With my savings from Singapore (where tax was low) and the sale of the MG Midget, I was able to stay in first-class hotels.

It was summer in the Northern hemisphere. In Mexico, I met a group of three young women from the USA. They were good company as we toured the tourist sites. At an English-speaking Church service I was moved to stay in Mexico and do mission work. I resisted, and flew to Los Angeles, where I stayed with a friend of Bruce's. He was gay, a teacher and a generous host. He showed me the sights, including Forest Lawn Cemetery where wealthy personalities and film stars are buried. It was started by a committed Christian who believed in a joyous life after death. As well as seeing the vaults and graves, Forest Lawn had a multimedia visual spectacular story of Jesus' resurrection. People would come to spend a day there.

In a side trip to San Francisco, I stumbled on the hippy scene, where the song, *Are you going to San Francisco*, kept going around and around in my brain. In another side trip, to Boston, I met a young US Marine, recently returned from Vietnam, who let me use his vouchers to stay in a five-star hotel. The US visit was an eye opener for someone who had spent two years in Singapore. The US culture was booming with talk-back radio, the personal growth movement like the Jesus People, Hare Krishna, plus the hippies, and it was the sexual revolution! I was excited to take a helicopter from the roof of the Pan Am Building to New York Airport, to fly to London.

I arrived in London in August 1966. An old friend from Jackson Wain in Sydney put me up in his Highgate apartment. He had a job at the number one agency in London - J. Walter Thompson. London was another culture shock. I was struck by how everything was so small compared to the United States - small buildings, rooms, cars. On my first day, I was walking around from Victoria Station and noticed a building that I thought I recognised, but thought was tiny - it was Buckingham Palace.

I planned to spend two years in London. Finding a job was difficult. In August, most people were on summer holidays. Jackson Wain, in London, a recently opened branch on Regent Street, had nothing for me. I was content to do any work to survive and applied as a night security guard. I was given the job, was allocated my companion, an Alsatian dog, and was told my uniform was on its way.

Fortunately, another job opportunity soon came via an Australian contact at Hobson, Bates & Partners, in their International Unit. I think I was given this job because of my time in Singapore, and because Australians were well regarded as good workers. HBP was the sixth largest agency in billings in the UK. Their Australian partner was George Patterson, the largest agency in Australia and owners of Cathay Advertising in Singapore. In October 1966, I put on my smart Singapore tailored suit, with a 32-inch waist, and arrived at the agency's modern office, near Euston Station.

The agency had been recently established to serve clients with overseas business. The largest one was British American Tobacco. Despite my objection to smoking and cigarette advertising, I succumbed to the mighty dollar (pound). I reasoned I would work on other accounts, so my conscience was relieved. It's amazing how sometimes you can reason anything you want.

Another account that appealed greatly to me was the first World Advertising Conference, involving advertising and marketing for the largest advertising conference, to be held in London in June 1967. This was a good account for a young Aussie. I met and worked with the Chairman of the Conference, Jack Wynne-Williams - CEO of the second largest agency in London, along with other top executives from other agencies.

HBP International was a small agency with about eight people. It was run by a tall, ex-Army man, Lieutenant-Colonel Colin Gray MBE, who had been under the command of Field Marshall General Bernard Montgomery at the Allies' first land victory at El Alamein, Egypt. Immaculately dressed in a three-piece tailored suit with an eye glass, Gray would call people 'Love'. He enjoyed travelling overseas and, no doubt, enjoyed female company. He had no idea about advertising. He had never worked in the advertising industry, but was General Manager of a popular theatre restaurant - 'Talk of the Town'. He was a good people person, a great leader and kept the clients happy. The agency had the Greek Tourist account. Colonel Gray enjoyed wining and dining the Greek Generals who ran their country.

The HBP London agency was taken over by the Ted Bates agency of New York, known for promoting its Unique Selling Proposition (USP). This concept, USP, referred to a promised benefit that only the product in question could deliver. If none could be found, one was invented.

John Hobson was a reserved man. His business partner, John Metcalf, ran the public relations operation and supervised our new outfit. I was impressed by his spartan office and his use of short sentences in letters and memos. I don't think John Hobson and John Metcalf got on well together.

Aussies were generally liked in the UK. They worked hard and played hard, and many who lived there did well when they returned to Australia. There was still a hint of class distinction. Most agency heads came from private schools. But younger creative copywriters and artists from working class backgrounds were joining agencies. It was a very progressive time.

I didn't want to live in Earls Court, where many Australians lived. Eventually, I answered an advert in the *Evening Standard* and found a room in a three-bedroom house in a tree-lined street at Golders Green, a suburb on the tube Northern Line, which had a large Jewish population. I shared the house with two English guys. The house was cold and dusty, and the bed was uncomfortable. The cultural shock of moving from Singapore and Australia to London wasn't the only thing I found difficult. The weather got me down, after the blue, cloudless skies of Singapore and Sydney.

I think I was depressed when I arrived, feeling burnout from the failed relationship in Singapore. Also, in Singapore I had been a big fish in a relatively small pond. The growth with new clients and the rapid rise from a staff of three to 33 in two years in Singapore was mind blowing! And that unique experience was going to be difficult to replicate.

'A wife of noble character who can find? She is more than rubies. Her husband has full confidence in her and lacks noting of value. She brings him good, not harm, all the days of her life.'
PROVERBS 31: 10-11 NIV

CHAPTER 12

LYNDA

Apart from my friend, Walter Knight I knew no-one else in London. So, looking for Christian fellowship, I attended the morning service at All Souls, Langham Place, London, opposite the BBC and up from Regent Street. All Souls was the leading Evangelical Anglican Church in Britain. When architect John Nash designed All Souls Church, consecrated in 1824, he was fulfilling a brief for one of several new Churches, and incorporated it into his grand plans for the area backed then by the Prince Regent.

John Stott had become the rector in 1950 and remained until 1975. He was an acknowledged academic theologian, writing more than fifty books on the Christian Faith. In 2005, *Time* magazine declared Stott to be one of the hundred most influential people in the world. His most famous book was *Basic Christianity*, which helped me in becoming a Christian in the early 1960s. All Souls attracted a lot of young people from around the world, particularly from Commonwealth countries. There were so many that All Souls held an evening meal with a speaker. It was known as the Wednesday Club - located off Oxford Street -

all very convenient. It was a place to meet new people and enjoy a meal and hear an interesting speaker.

But there was more waiting for me on my third visit to the Wednesday Club. That chance would change my life forever. Standing in front of the map of the world, tall, blonde, dressed in a mini skirt (this was the swinging sixties) and, in accordance with the universal practice of Churches, fixing ribbons from the UK to countries where missionaries were serving, stood my future wife! Her name was Lynda Anne Wyatt. She was twenty years old. Her parents and her sisters, Christina and Sheila, had moved from West London to Salisbury, in Wiltshire, because her father had a new job as a time and motion manager at Sadia Water Heaters. He was in charge of one hundred women. He was a good-looking man. What a job he had!

Lynda didn't want to live in Salisbury and moved to London. She had answered an ad to share a flat with two other young women, and went to live in Grosvenor Place, not far from Baker Street Station, London. She was working at Butlins Holiday Camps head office in Oxford Street (opposite Selfridges Department Store) as secretary to Sir William Butlins's Personal Assistant. Later she worked as secretary to the Company's Solicitor. Butlins was a most popular destination holiday before cheap flights and holiday packages to Spain were introduced in the late '60s. It was a very structured holiday, with the famed Red Coats entertaining the holiday makers.

It was Lynda's first week, and like me, had attended All Souls, and decided to check out the Wednesday Club. I wandered over in my casual relaxed manner, introduced myself and discovered that she lived in Grosvenor Place, a walking distance away, and

LYNDA

on the bus route to my digs at Golders Green! Lynda thought I was one of the organisers.

I walked Lynda home. A few days later, I started the job at HBP and phoned Lynda to join me for dinner to celebrate. We continued seeing each other and, early in our relationship, I told Lynda that I already had plans to return to Sydney in October 1968. In February 1967, I arranged a party for Lynda to celebrate her twenty-first birthday at the house in Wentworth Avenue, Golders Green. This was a happy event although I noticed one young man, a former boyfriend, was chatting to Lynda - I was jealous. But it turned out there was no reason to be jealous, as he was telling Lynda that he had found a new girlfriend.

Lynda's father, Syd, served in WWII. In 1941 he volunteered to join a special branch of the Army and was accepted as a corporal. Their role was to be parachuted or flown in wooden gliders to behind enemy lines. After training, as qualified airborne soldiers, they were given red berets to wear and were known as the 1st Air Landing Brigade of the 1st Airborne Division. Later, they were nicknamed, the 'Red Devils' by the Germans. On 17 September 1944, their mission was to capture a bridge over the river Rhine at Arnhem in Holland. Arnhem Bridge was thirty miles behind the enemy lines.

Known as 'Operation Market Garden' it was conceived by Field Marshal Sir Bernard Montgomery, who believed a successful assault to secure bridges would reduce the war by six months. He was mistaken. The operation was a failure, as the Germans discovered what was about to happen and were prepared. Fierce fighting followed and it was remembered as The Battle of Arnhem. Syd was wounded in the leg by shrapnel.

He was moved to Elizabeth Hospital, Arnhem, and was interned as a prisoner of war. Years later, he told Lynda he had a spiritual experience, while he was laying injured in the thick of the fighting, he saw a glowing light, which he believed was God with him. Syd was released from the German prisoner of war camp at the end of the War, after six months' captivity. He returned home to England in April 1945 and was confirmed in the Anglican Church. He and his wife, Rose, made a home and had a family of three daughters. Lynda and I spent the Easter that year in Amsterdam and visited St Elizabeth Hospital in Arnhem.

At the Wednesday Club, I also met Ian Kemp Tucker, who became a good friend. He had a car and liked to drive and, having failed my London driver's test, I was happy for him to be my chauffeur. Ian was brought up in the Seventh Day Adventist Faith but found the narrow, fundamentalist approach suffocating.

We were fortunate that there were outstanding Christian speakers in the London Churches. Apart from Rev John Stott at All Souls, there was Rev Martyn Lloyd Jones, a Welshman, at Westminster Chapel. He was a successful author and preacher from the John Calvin Reformed wing, another group that held a black and white view of the Bible.

Next, was Dr Leslie Weatherhead - again, a popular author, but in the liberal Protestant tradition, and a long-time minister at City Temple Church. His approach was highly emotional - rich in God's grace. Then there was Rev Howard Williams, another Welshman, who was the Baptist pastor at Bloomsbury Baptist Church. Howard was a likeable man, a liberal who preached sermons that made you think.

So, it depended on our mood on a Sunday evening. If we wanted a good expository sermon with Bible references, it was John Stott. If we wanted a more fundamental, black and white view of the Bible, we heard Rev Martyn Lloyd James. Then, if we needed a more liberal, emotional, people-centred sermon, Weatherhead and Williams would do the trick.

On 8 July 1967, when Lynda and I had been seeing each other for nearly nine months, we dined at our favourite Italian restaurant Bertorelli, in Charlotte Street, and I proposed to her. Lynda accepted my proposal of marriage, and we toasted each other and then found the post office to send telegrams to our families.

Happily, Lynda loved the idea of returning with me to live in Australia and looked forward to this adventure.

We were married in a tiny, 800-year-old Church of England church, St Laurence in Old Sarum, Salisbury, near Stonehenge on 21 October 1967. The vicar, in welcoming the Congregation, said, 'In this church, which has seen many marriages over the past eight hundred years, I welcome you'. Eight hundred years, Wow! Unfortunately, most of my family couldn't attend the wedding, except for my cousin Cheryl.

A week before the wedding, I was an organiser at a conference of BAT executives at an exclusive conference centre near London. They were a good bunch and gave me a wedding present.

However, I became anxious and my underlying depression worsened. I was depressed after the engagement and before the wedding. Was I doing the right thing? Will the marriage last? My parent's marriage had been far from happy. It caused panic attacks if a train I was travelling on stopped in a tunnel. I sought counselling to deal with my mood, and was prescribed Valium again.

Fortunately, my mood lifted after the wedding and during our honeymoon in Majorca in late October. Lynda saw a new Tom - no longer sombre, quiet and introverted, but a laughing, happier, extroverted Tom. Whom have I married, she thought? It's like Dr Jekyll and Mr Hyde!

Lynda and I rented a flat in Golders Green, where I had lived, and later a flat at North Finchley. In addition to hearing sermons from the famous preachers and authors like Stott, Lloyd Jones, Weatherhead and Williams on Sunday evenings, we attended the morning service at a nearby Open Brethren Church, which is not to be confused with the closed Plymouth Brethren Church sect. Here was a fine group of friendly, sincere people. The sermons were outstanding, preached by a lay person and not an ordained minister. It was a nice change.

The job at Hobson Bates & Partners was interesting and challenging. My major accounts included the first International Advertising Conference and, as the agency appointed by the Conference Committee, I managed the account. Another account was British Travel, aimed at attracting tourists from Australia, New Zealand, Brazil, Argentina and South Africa. But the major client, and the reason for setting up the International Division, was British American Tobacco. The task was to create campaigns for non-UK markets for brands like Lucky Strike, Pall Mall and the world's first 100mm cigarette, DuMaurier.

For an Australian working for a large international agency, it was a wonderful opportunity to travel in Europe, as I had done in Singapore with Malaysian Singapore Airlines, visiting South East Asian cities.

I enjoyed coordinating the BAT brands in Paris, Oslo, Stockholm, Madrid and Lisbon. I would visit the local agency and plan the campaigns with them as well as seeing the tourist sites. The local agency people would take me for lunch and dinner. All generous expenses paid for - a good life.

Although I didn't smoke and was against smoking, I used the standard, cop out explanation, 'if it's legal, it can be advertised'. The client had unlimited funds. An American was imported to direct the expensive cinema and TV commercials.

My Christian Faith and participation, felt minimal for two years. Although I helped at summer camps for private school boys, attended a Billy Graham Crusade, and heard and met a few of London's leading ministers. I missed having more involvement of service and helping Churches and Christian ministries to be more effective using the techniques of modern marketing.

Although I had a good job and recently married, I felt like a fish out of water. I didn't feel at home in London. I had decided to spend two years there. Perhaps, I thought, things would improve when we returned to Sydney.

'If you are brave enough to say goodbye life will reward you with a new hello.'
PAULO COELHO

CHAPTER 13

LEAVING LONDON

Lynda and I did a lot of sightseeing. We knew we were eventually returning to Australia, so we did as much as we could while still in London. We climbed over the fallen stones at Stonehenge, visited museums and art galleries, and saw the sites. We did a hitchhiking tour of Britain and Wales, where we found the drivers helpful. They loved to point out the attractions of their towns.

The month before we left England to go back to Australia to live, Lynda and I joined a young people's camping trip, for thirty days, around Western Europe. There were three minibuses. Our tour leader and his drivers were all Australian. This tour was to be their last one, after three years of driving young travellers, mainly Australians, around Europe, before they all returned home. Of course, they'd made many friends at the camping sites of Europe and we soon discovered that, at each camp site, the Australians were given a farewell party. Next morning, they were somewhat hungover, so it was pretty nerve wrecking to be driven through the frantic streets of Italy, and especially on the day we were to climb the Brenner Pass. That caused the tourists on each bus to call for a halt and we all slept the night in a barn in a field, somewhere in the Alps.

We took our time travelling back to Australia from England, visiting Greece, Israel, India, Hong Kong, Malaysia, Singapore and Indonesia.

When our plane landed in Tel Aviv, we made our way to our hotel. As we were booking in we chatted to a fellow passenger, an older woman from Tasmania, who had been travelling on her own, booking into hotels along the way. Unfortunately, our hotel told her that they were fully booked and so was the rest of Tel Aviv, owing to a huge convention taking place. We were worried for her and suggested she could stay with us in our room, asking the staff to put a roller-bed for her in our room. She was incredibly grateful and said she hadn't relished the thought of going back to the airport to sleep in the airport lounge.

Lynda and I were only happy that we could help her. I remember seeing this lady kneel down beside her bed in prayer. We didn't like to mention to her that this night was our first wedding anniversary!

The next day at Tel Aviv airport, we couldn't help but notice all the bullet holes in the airport walls. This was soon after the six-day war in 1967. There was something going on at the airport that we couldn't figure out. Seeing official looking people running around, Lynda and I weren't the only ones to be nervous about the unknown. General Moshe Dayan and his bodyguards came into the departure lounge. I was terrified. 'What if there is a bomb on board? What if terrorists would attack us?' I spoke to two English speaking Catholic priests about my fears. They too were frightened. We flew to New Delhi thinking the General was on the plane. But he wasn't. He had come to the airport to farewell his wife who was flying with us to India. We didn't know this. The flight was the most terrifying one I have ever had, but we were on our way to Sydney, ready for a fresh new start!

'Chase your dreams but always know the road will lead you home again.'
ZIAD K. ABDELNOUR

CHAPTER 14

HOME

Lynda and I arrived in Sydney in December 1968 and were warmly welcomed by Mum, Dad and Bruce. We found a flat in a large house at Northwood on the Lane Cove River.

It felt strange to me, and it was a big change for Lynda. I had been away for four years and Australia had changed. It was more prosperous. The population, then 12 million, was half of what it is today. The following year came a mining boom (started by Poseidon Nickel), which then burst in 1970.

I tried to reconnect with old friends and to find places where I could serve in Christian ministry. We joined North Sydney Baptist Church where Rev Norm Chambers was the pastor. Before that, he was the pastor I had known at Dulwich Hill Baptist Church.

My old boss, Frank Grace at Jackson Wain (now owned by Leo Burnett, Chicago), contacted me and offered me a job, which I accepted. I became a senior account executive, with a large office and a secretary, but I didn't feel at home. I worked on one of the largest accounts, Sunbeam Appliances, which was run by some arrogant and unpleasant executive staff. But it was a big account and I worked well with the Advertising Manager.

It's said that you shouldn't go back to an old job. I think FEG still regarded me as a young man in his early twenties. Now at age 27, I called him 'Frank', but was told by one of his associates I should call him 'Mr Grace'.

John Adams, whom I had known in the earlier years at Jackson Wain, was working at J. Walter Thompson, then the second largest agency in Australia. He phoned and offered me a job handling the Bonds clothing business and a few Lever & Kitchen brands. I jumped at the opportunity and joined JWT in 1971. FEG was upset when I resigned, and tried to talk me out of it by saying that JWT creative people were on drugs. I think he was genuinely concerned about my future.

So, I moved from the Jackson Wain office in North Sydney to JWT, who were in an older building in Elizabeth Street, opposite Mark Foy's Department Store, next to The Salvation Army headquarters. J. Walter Thompson was a big change. It was the largest agency in the world. The Sydney office, established in 1930, was the second largest in Australia, was professionally managed, and had a blue-chip list of clients.

My JWT clients were great. We would lunch with them regularly at top restaurants. At JWT, I felt we were part of a great tradition. It was one of the world's oldest agencies, started in 1896. We were JWT people, and we wore JWT cuff links. I visited JWT London in 1973 for an international conference with other international JWT branches, sponsored by Unilever.

Unlike Frank Grace, the Chairman, John Sharman, was hardly seen. I had met him in New York when I was travelling to London. John was one of the top people in the JWT world. They attracted good people. They believed in training, research and keeping up with changes in society. The agency had a library with the latest books and magazines on marketing. One of the first training courses I did was on Self Organisation, a series of five sessions. I would learn a lot at JWT, and some of it would be life changing.

'Communication is the most important skill in life.'
STEPHEN COVEY

CHAPTER 15

HOW ADVERTISING WORKS

In the early 1970s, JWT employed Hugh Mackay to run a series of educational seminars on the subject, 'How Does Advertising Work?'

Hugh was an up-and-coming young social psychologist and researcher who conducted regular surveys of public opinion on a wide range of topics. He had been a pioneer in the development of qualitative research methods in Australia, using individual, in-depth interviews and small group discussions, to generate spontaneous conversation about the topics he was studying, rather than asking prescribed questions. He had started his own research and consulting business in 1971.

He was also a specialist in the psychology of communication, and would go on to establish The Centre for Communication Studies, in Bathurst and write a book called *Why Don't People Listen?*, which was published in 1994.

I took in every word Hugh said at these seminars. I had been raised to regard advertising in military terms - we used words like strategy, objectives, execution, targets, etc. That seemingly aggressive approach was described by Hugh as the 'injection' model of communication, where you think of your message as being rather like a potent drug, and the medium as being like the syringe you use to inject your message into the brain of your unsuspecting audience. On that model, all you would need to do was inject the message in sufficient quantities and with sufficient frequency and your audience would be influenced to think what you wanted them to think, to feel what you wanted them to feel and - even better! - do what you wanted them to do (like buy the product or service you were promoting). 'Completely wrong', Hugh said, 'The injection theory simply doesn't work'. He pointed out that if it really was that simple, we would be constantly changing our minds in response to every persuasive message that reached our brains.

By contrast, Hugh explained to us, that the alleged 'power' of advertising lies with the audience, not the message. One of the most memorable things he taught us was: 'It's not what the message does to the audience but what the audience does with the message, which determines the outcome of the communication'. The implication of that was mind-blowing to people raised on the 'injection' model. It meant that the starting point for effective advertising - or effective communication of any kind - is to get inside the mind of the audience, so as to know their existing attitudes and predispositions. Hugh used the metaphor of the 'cage', explaining that we all exist within a framework of attitudes, values and beliefs, built up through our personal experiences, acting as a kind of protective barrier against messages that are incompatible with these existing attitudes. We all feel secure and comfortable within our own personal 'mind-cages' because we have built them to suit ourselves.

And here's the most important part: from inside our own mind-cages, we see the world through the filter of our own beliefs - like looking out a window through the slats of a Venetian blind - the slats shape the view, and are, in fact, part of the view. The metaphorical cage explains why we are so good at twisting, filtering and interpreting messages we don't agree with, or that challenge us to change our minds - the phenomenon psychologists call 'selective perception'. Above all, we seek reinforcement of our existing attitudes, values and beliefs, which point to one of the most important roles that advertising (or any other form of communication, including religious communication) can play - maintaining attitudes, values and beliefs, when preaching to the converted!

This means that, to be effective, advertising must position itself to respond to the existing attitudes of the audience; to align the message with their existing predispositions; and to show them how this product or service can make their existing dreams come true!

At that time - and perhaps even today - the 'injection' model of communication was alive and well in the Church. I remember a well-meaning, dedicated Deacon saying all we had to do was to get people to read tracts and they would become Christians. If only it were so easy!

In a 1970s paper, 'Communication problems of the organised Church', Hugh wrote, 'What is communication? The creation of common ground (or a feeling of affinity) between a communicator and their audience.' He explained how messages that try to attack existing attitudes, head-on, are most likely to produce precisely the opposite result - not just failing in their aim, but actually reinforcing the very attitudes they are trying to change. Hugh says the best way to reinforce someone's existing attitudes is to attack them!

Effective communication must therefore be undertaken from the audience's point of view. For the Church, communication must begin with the sympathetic understanding of the community's point of view on any subject relevant to Christian communication. It doesn't mean we have to accept other people's points of view, but it does mean we have to accept that that is their point of view. We have to work within the framework of the audience's 'cage'. The Church must get inside the community's point of view and work from that, as if it were the Church's own. For example: the Church needs to understand the 'experience generation' (where 'being, doing, feeling and experiencing' outweigh 'saying' and 'authority').

Repeatedly, Hugh Mackay emphasised that the most effective channel of communication - by far - is the channel of our personal relationships. Even when there's a big advertising budget for a particular brand, a personal recommendation from a friend or family member, or even from a salesperson, will generally outweigh the effect of that media advertising. This is now seen in today's media environment, where social media tends to be more influential than mass media, precisely because social media feels more personal.

I have followed Hugh's career by attending many of his presentations and reading his non-fiction books over the years. (I admit only reading two of his fiction books.) His latest non-fiction book, *The Inner Self: The Joy Of Discovering Who We Are*, speaks to the many readers interested in personal growth. Hugh covers his own personal journey, including his mid-life crisis and the challenge to find the True Self from the False Self. I write about these insights in later chapters.

From Hugh's work, I can see three important messages for the Church. Firstly, church services provide a significant source of reinforcement of the Faith of committed Christians, though even here we often fail to relate to the audience's point of view. What we know about the psychology of communication should lead us to place more emphasis on pastoral work, as a constant source of 'research' for preachers and other Church leaders. We need to know what people are thinking and feeling, on a continuous basis. The best sermons - like the best ads - are a response to the needs of the Congregation.

Secondly, the mass media offer a tempting (but frequently self-deluded) opportunity. Their role will almost inevitably be that of a reinforcer rather than a converter. Does 'preaching' have a role in mass communication? Or is this the place for moral teaching through the production of programmes that are not overtly Christian? When will the Church produce films with a Christian theme, like the academy award winning films, *Chariots of Fire* or *The Mission*?

Finally, the Church's golden opportunity is in inter-personal (rather than mass-media) communication. Most advertisers would give anything for the communication manpower available within the Church. Personal influence remains the most effective of all: the Church needs to gear itself to this channel of communication much more effectively, before looking for 'second-best' opportunities within the channels of mass media.

'Transformed people transform people.'
RICHARD ROHR

CHAPTER 16

FEMINISM AND FILM STARS

Another interesting speaker was Ita Buttrose, then an editor of a JWT client, Consolidated Press, who published the *Australian Women's Weekly* - the top circulation magazine per capita in the world. Ita came to talk to the audience, consisting of predominantly men (there were very few female account handlers), about the launching of a new women's magazine called *Cleo*.

'*Cleo* is the start of the Women's Movement', she enthusiastically proclaimed. The first issue had a double page spread of a young and handsome Jack Thompson, naked, with his hand appropriately placed, in a token of modesty. Aimed at women aged 20 to 40, it was frank about sexuality. *Cleo* was modelled largely on the US magazine *Cosmopolitan*, after the Packer family lost the rights to the latter title to rivals, Fairfax. Kerry Packer wanted to start his own magazine as a competitor to *Cosmopolitan*.

The audience at JWT were impressed. Up till then, most married women didn't work: their lives were as good housewives who, when they had left school in the fifties and sixties, became secretaries, nurses, or teachers.

Ita said that the personality of the Australian woman was rapidly changing. This was an era when hopes for social and political changes were high. *Cleo*, Ita continued, 'was a welcome addition for women aged between 20 and 40 who were looking for something more than the recipes, knitting tips and coverage of the Royal Family'. Launched in November 1972, *Cleo's* circulation reached 200,000 copies.

Ita continued to have a spectacular career in the media. Having edited the *Australian Women's Weekly*, she started her own magazine *Ita*, and worked for both Kerry Packer and Rupert Murdoch. She is now Chair of the ABC.

Ita's comments on the Women's Movement struck a chord with me. I knew Virginia Slims cigarette brand was launched in America in 1968 with the slogan, 'You've come a long way, baby'. Helen Reddy had recorded *I am Woman* in 1972, which became the anthem for the growing Women's Movement. Germaine Greer's novel, *The Female Eunuch*, was published in 1970. This book became an international best seller and was an important and revolutionary breakthrough for all society, not just the feminist movement. Her book challenged the role of Australian housewives, which Greer believed led to repression.

Greer believed strongly that male dominance of business, politics, law and the media resulted in gender inequality. It certainly was the case in advertising.

I tried to relate this trend to my clients who had women as their target audience. My main account was Bonds - of Chesty Bond fame. (Interesting that my parents had met while working at Bonds.) It was one of JWT's biggest and oldest clients. Women bought most of their husband's underwear. The client was wonderful. The executive team were real gentlemen - it was a privilege to deal with them. We made two presentations to Bonds each year. The main one was in August for the spring summer promotion, the other was in March. I would fly to both Melbourne and Brisbane to present the campaigns to the client.

The other client I worked on was Lever & Kitchen which had several brands - Lux Toilet Soap, Lux Liquid and Handy Andy. Lever & Kitchen products were frequently bought by women. A division of Unilever, L & K relied heavily on marketing which included research. Their marketing people were called brand managers, who were university trained and would provide their agencies with well prepared creative briefs. The agency would respond with a document setting out their understanding of what was required. A lot of people think advertisements and TV spots are based on a simple creative idea in a vacuum - no! All the work I have done is based on a number of objectives and agreed strategies before the copywriter and artist do their bit. Sometimes, two creative teams will work on the assignment before research is done, to see if the commercial appeals to the target audience.

With L & K they had two large international agencies with allocated brands. We would compete with the other agency to win new assignments. So, creativity and product sales were vital. Each month, we would gather to hear the results of the sales by a well-respected research company. Before I left JWT, we gained the L & K Solvol soap account - a personal coup.

Lux Toilet Soap had been created in 1929 with attractive, female, Hollywood stars endorsing the product. Lux pioneered the trend of celebrity product endorsement.

For bigger stars, JWT would send a film crew to London to satisfy the local union demands of not using commercials produced overseas. It was a free trip to do nothing but watch the filming. They were known as 'ghost crews'.

As there was no international filming taking place at this time, we imported two of our own stars. Both had appeared in films and TV. They were highly attractive and, at the time, were well known by Australian women. One star was Susan Strasberg, daughter of well-known method actor teacher, Lee Strasberg. She was a delight and a small group of us, with our wives, dined with her at a restaurant at The Gap at Watson's Bay. The other star was Linda Crystal, star of the TV series, *The High Chaparral*. We had planned her commercial to be filmed out at Windsor, a small distance from Sydney.

At midday, I received a call from the director to say Linda had fallen from her horse and had been taken to Hawkesbury Hospital. I quickly read the contract to see if our client and JWT were covered by insurance. I imagined the headlines, 'Hollywood actress sues soap manufacturer and its agency for five million dollars!' I visited her in hospital, smiling and clutching a bouquet of red roses. Fortunately, Linda's fall wasn't serious, and she continued the filming.

JWT had several creative people who went on to bigger things:

Richard Walsh, worked as a creative group head from 1968 to 1970. Earlier, he co-founded and co-edited the controversial *OZ* magazine in Australia and London. He was founder of *POL* magazine and edited the *National Review*, before joining Angus and Robertson, and then Kerry Packer's Australian Consolidated Press.

Bryce Courtney, left JWT and became a world-famous author with his first best-selling book, *The Power of One*. Bryce was a popular speaker at conferences. He had a flamboyant entrance. Striding towards the lectern, he would take off his blazer and throw it dramatically on the floor.

Ken Done, the artist who worked with me on the Bonds account, was a fantastic person to work with. Ken established a look and style with vibrant colours, loved by thousands of Japanese tourists. Ken had sponsored Llewellyn Thomas from London, where they both worked at JWT, again the top agency in London. Llew was the son of the famous author Dylan Thomas. I think Llew probably enjoyed coming to Sydney, away from the memory of his Dad, who died tragically in 1953, aged thirty-nine, because of heavy drinking. Ken and I met recently at a reception to launch his memoir, *A Life Coloured In*. Despite a prostate cancer scare and a financial swindle, Ken is now doing well.

I was now thirty-two, an age at which many people open their own businesses. I was ambitious and restless. By this time, I had enough experience (I'd had sixteen years in advertising), and I was mature enough to do my own thing. If I moved again to another top agency, it would be like changing the colour of the carpet. There would be similar clients, planning concepts, similar politics and, more importantly, by the time I turned forty, I thought I would be past my use-by date. Advertising agencies chewed up many people and spat them out by this age.

I thought it was time to move on and do my own thing. But should I leave a supportive, happy agency with good clients like Pan Am, a promising future, with trips to London and to the

Pacific Islands? Also I had to consider my responsibility to the family. Our son, Michael had been born a year earlier. I had a mortgage and little cash. This was to be a big decision. I thought and prayed through the possible pitfalls, failures and stress, and humiliation from family and friends.

'Strength and growth come only through continuous effort and struggle.'
NAPOLEON HILL

CHAPTER 17

TOM GLYNN ADVERTISING (TGA)

Should I decide to open my own agency? There were risks. Most new advertising agencies had an account man (suit) and a creative person as partners. They had worked on the client's account before launching their own business.

I knew some were not successful. People starting their own agency tend to need big egos. Obviously, I had to have a strong ego, too.

I didn't have clients who would join me. There was no way clients at JWT, like Bonds, Lever & Kitchen, or Pan Am would join a new one-man agency (although I did receive a project later from Bonds for a series of posters), which put 'a cat among the pigeons' when JWT discovered it in a four page insert promoting our clients which we had placed in *Broadcasting and Television*, the industry trade journal.

I wanted to move from selling products to a person, Jesus Christ. I saw an opportunity, as many Christian ministries and charities were struggling. In 1973, interest rates were around 12% and charities' donations were down.

My friend from Dulwich Hill Baptist Church, Ken Harrison, had left the Anglican Home Mission Society (now Anglicare) as Communications and Fundraising Manager and they were looking to replace him.

On my return from London, I became a committee member for promoting the Scripture Union, which was also struggling to raise funds. I felt frustrated on leaving the monthly meetings with the misleading thought, that a new leaflet would magically increase their funds. It needed a new view and a complete overview of their operations.

The Scripture Union was known for its well-produced and popular Bible reading notes. It also ran CSSM - Children's Special Service Missions - now called Beach Missions. Volunteers (mainly young Christians) from different Churches went on a mission together, setting up large tents at beaches for two weeks during the Christmas holidays. They arranged daily programmes for the children of campers. The keen participants believed they were influencing children for Christianity - and they did, remarkably well. But I also believed the greater benefit was in building their own Faith and, sometimes, finding a Christian partner. The initials, CSSM became known to some as 'Come single, soon married'. This happened with a couple Lynda and I have now known for many years.

I have always believed a person, or an organisation, should review themselves every three years, because of the rapid and continuous change in our society. I saw the opportunity for a new business model and service. I would open an agency and serve both the Anglican Home Mission Society (AHMS) and the Scripture Union (SU), based on a monthly fee, with an added service fee on all creative material produced by the agency.

The monthly fee was not large. It was a lot less than employing a staff person, and was enough income to get me through the first three months. And we both had an option - if the relationships were not working, either partner could cancel the agreement.

I submitted proposals setting out the benefits to both groups to use TGA as consultants rather than each employing a person who had marketing, public relations, fundraising and advertising experience. They both said they would phone me, coincidentally on the same night, to tell me of their decision. There were three options: first, both would reject the submission, leaving me at JWT. Second, one would accept, the other decline - and what would I do then? Third, both would accept.

I waited anxiously for the phone calls. First, AHMS phoned - 'You're on!' The second call from SU, 'We accept your proposal. Congratulations!' I was over the moon! I saw God's lead in this. There was another Christian group, Pilgrim Art Studio, whose three partners were Sydney Anglicans. Pilgrim had been serving both these and other Christian organisations on a job-by-job basis.

My approach was a brand-new model for these Christian organisations - a monthly fee paid to an outside consulting agency.

God's other 'raindrops from heaven' came when I met the manager of my local NAB branch, at the corner of Pitt and Bathurst Streets, Sydney, to arrange an overdraft. 'What can I do for you?' he asked. 'I need a $10,000 loan to open an agency', I replied. 'That's a risky business, Tom. What clients do you have?' he enquired. Feeling a little embarrassed, I said, 'No clients you would know - religious ones - the Anglican Home Mission Society and the Scripture Union'. 'I know them both', he replied, grinning. 'I'm the Chairman of Anglican Home Mission Society Op Shops - and both of them bank with us. How much do you want?' This was the second incident to show me I was being guided by God.

There were not many Christians working in the media. The *Sydney Morning Herald* covered Church activities, and their religious correspondent, Alan Gill, did a fine job from 1971-1988. There were few people in advertising. Over the years, I would contact younger Christians in the industry to encourage them in their careers.

I had used the months before leaving JWT imagining I was running my own business. I read books on establishing a new business. I had an exercise book in which I wrote down insights and principles under the headings, A to Z. I needed to be prepared! Ken Done kindly designed the letterhead and stationery - and he didn't charge me!

I resigned from JWT and leased an office a few doors down in Elizabeth Street, past the Salvation Army, in the recently renovated Metters building. Just in case, if it wasn't successful, I could return to JWT. 'Mother' (J. Walter Thompson) would take me back.

'Ask and It will be given to you; seek and you will find; knock and the door will be opened to you.'
MATTHEW 7:7 NIV

CHAPTER 18

DREAM FULFILLED

Tom Glynn Advertising opened its doors on 3 February 1974, with Lynda Glynn as secretary and typist. Our one-year old son, Michael, was parked in his cot in the tiny office with room for about four desks. An architect friend, Ridley Smith, suggested I partition the area with a hung print fabric. There was no air conditioning. I had bought second-hand furniture.

I discussed joining with a partner, a freelance copywriter, with whom I had worked at Jackson Wain and JWT. I wasn't confident of having partners because of my need to be in control. I had decided to use my name, Tom Glynn, for the agency name. I thought I was in good company. Many top agencies were named after their founders, like, George Patterson, Leo Burnett, Ted Bates and J. Walter Thompson.

I decided it was wise not to *go* into business but to *grow* into the business. The failure rate of new businesses is sobering. 20% fail in their first year, 30% fail in their second year, 50% fail within five years. Only 30% of small businesses are still operating after ten years. I wanted to be included in this group.

After a few weeks, with Lynda finding it difficult to help, I appointed a secretary and personal assistant, who was a wonderful help.

I had two foundation clients, AHMS and SU. My approach of servicing them as an outside consultant was entirely new. From my point of view, I would not get caught up with their internal politics and could be a 'maverick' and 'stirrer' to question and to encourage new things. More companies were using consultants.

I had decided to also attract commercial clients to keep me up to date in the advertising industry and provide added income to grow the agency. I chose Church clients, partly because of my commitment to God, but also I thought, to lessen my chances of rejection - the problem I had always faced.

There were only a few fundraising consultants at the time. We became the first fundraising agency to work with Christian organisations.

Since coming to Faith when I was twenty-one, I saw that the Church and Christian organisations were not using the principles and techniques of modern marketing and advertising. The charities and Church groups thought more about what they do, than how they do. They were also struggling with high interest rates, declining income and lack of suitably trained executives in marketing, promotion and fundraising. They were sincere and would pray, but sincerity alone would not improve their situation. There were deep structural and historic beliefs and practices that, I believed, were limiting the growth of Christian ministries.

The first few months were busy servicing my two clients. Fortunately, they were situated close together - AHMS in St Andrews House in George Street, and SU in nearby York Street.

I prepared a yearly marketing and fundraising program and produced the monthly newsletters, fundraising appeals and literature. I used the JWT's planning procedure, known as the 'T' Target Plan, in my documents:
1. What are we selling?
2. To whom are we selling?
3. How are we selling?
4. When are we selling?

In late 1974, a writer, a Christian from a top Sydney advertising agency, joined me as Creative Director. Sadly, we fell out and he left.

In June 1975, an artist joined me. We were accredited by the Media Council as an advertising agent to receive 10% commission on all media placements, printing etc. The standard service fee added was 7.5%. With artwork produced by the agency, the income was about 20%.

With no copywriter, Ross Meillon joined me as Creative Director. I had known Ross for a few years. Ross was working at John Clemenger Advertising and was servicing several Christian clients who followed him to TGA. John Clemenger's mother was a Christian and encouraged her son to take on religious accounts.

At TGA, we worked on other Church projects as well. For 23 years, TGA produced the annual report to be distributed in May at the annual festival held at the Sydney Town Hall. A dinner was held, followed by a meeting with a well-known speaker. At the first meeting, I believed this tradition would eventually end because the ageing audience from Sydney Churches would die, leaving the 2,500 seat Town Hall empty. I was wrong. The audience was replaced by other folk in their later years attending the Festival. The cycle continued.

One interesting project was from the NSW Council of Churches, which wanted to run newspaper advertisements calling for people to sign a petition objecting to Sunday hotel trading. Other Church projects included a TV Campaign for Force 10 and the Australian Council of Churches/Catholic Relief Overseas. It was designed to attract sponsors to their overseas aid program, and featured popular TV personality, Johnny Young. The test campaign ran in Adelaide but, sadly, was not successful.

I knew the power of using well known personalities in TV commercials. At JWT, I arranged for two American actresses to appear in TV commercials. Later Roger Climpson, a top TV broadcaster, appeared in a film for AHMS. The short ten-minute film started with Roger coming off the Channel 7 set after the news, saying 'there was a lot of bad news tonight'. His cameraman replied, 'Yes, but there was a lot of good news too, with a charity called Anglican Home Mission Society doing some great work. Why don't you investigate?' Roger did. The resulting film was well produced and shown in Churches.

As mentioned later, we used another well-known identity, Liberace, in August 1974 to promote Thomas Organs. This campaign was so successful, that we were able to move to larger premises in a new building in Mount Street, North Sydney. I had a window office with a view to the harbour. Sadly, this building was replaced later by new buildings.

Ken Harrison, the former Communications Manager at AHMS, joined us in 1977 as General Manager. Ken had a fascinating life, which he records in his self-published autobiography, *The View From My Bathtub*. He joined me to work on a new client, Sydney City Mission and we started a new venture, PIC - Public Interest Communications - as a public relations offshoot.

At TGA we were keen to get publicity promoting the agency, even if it were controversial. As the saying goes, 'any publicity is good publicity'.

Ken wrote and produced a Christmas commercial for Sydney City Mission, which became problematic. It involved the Executive Director, Charles Chambers and assistant Executive Director, Merle Hurcombe, driving around inner Sydney looking for children who may be in need. The car was well signed to show it was an official Mission vehicle.

The two spoke to a young girl sitting in the gutter. However, the fear about stranger danger was a hot topic. People were afraid of children being abducted. Six people objected to it and complained to the *Daily Mirror*, who made a big splash of the story. The commercial was banned by the Television Council. However, after many deputations to the Council, thankfully they agreed to let the commercial run after nine pm - what a relief.

We were booming but another controversy was to follow.

'For God did not give us a spirit of timidity, but a spirit of power, of love and of self-discipline.'
2 TIMOTHY 1:7 NIV

CHAPTER 19

CONTROVERSY

Sydney City Mission held a conference called 'Operation Understanding', promoting awareness of alcohol abuse. Ken invited Dana Andrews, a film star during Hollywood's Golden Years, having appeared in popular films such as, *The Best Years of Our Lives, A Walk in the Sun, The Oxbow Incident, Boomerang,* and *Laura*. He had also been President of the Screen Actors Guild. As a recovered alcoholic, Dana Andrews spoke with authority about alcoholism and its devastating effect on people suffering from this insidious disease.

Ken spoke and said TV liquor advertising was brainwashing our children. He said, 'The depiction of sporting heroes in liquor advertisements is most dangerous. When I ask my children what they feel like, they instantly say - "I feel like a Tooheys"', quoting the jingle in the commercial from one of the best-selling beers.

Ken kept going, 'An independent study found the Tooheys commercial was the most popular children's commercial in 1978. An advertising industry without a conscious is as harmless as a bath full of sharks.' It was heavy stuff.

We sent a press release to the media about the conference, including Ken's speech. It was widely covered. One Sydney daily newspaper captioned their article with, 'Put a stopper on TV grog, says ad-man'.

This particular article put the cat among the pigeons. The Advertising Federation of Australia, of which TGA was a member, and the Media Council of Australia, who controlled our accreditation, both wrote to me, criticising our comments and warning possible repercussions if we didn't follow the standard, 'If it's legal, it's OK to advertise'.

By now, I think many companies and agencies, some of which were our competitors, recognised TGA as a Christian/religious agency. That didn't stop our growth. Clients respected our predominantly ethical stance on social issues. We had a few putdowns, which hurt me. John Adams, a good friend who found me the job at JWT asked me if I was calling the agency 'Temple Advertising'? The other time was a presentation to the Sydney Holden Dealers, to win their advertising account worth many thousands of dollars. Our client, Sundell Motors Chatswood, put our name forward. We were one of three agencies presenting (or in our jargon, 'pitching'). At question time, after our successful presentation to about a dozen Holden dealers, one dealer, Tony Packard, sarcastically asked, 'Aren't you the religious, Christian agency?' I replied 'Yes'. We didn't get that account. I felt vindicated many years later, when Packard who'd become an MP, was charged over the use of concealed listening devices and forced to resign from Parliament in 1993. His dealership no longer exists.

Ken Harrison became so involved with Sydney City Mission that he felt frustrated he couldn't do more, and so he decided to join the Mission as a staff member. I recall going into his office to see him drawing a red heart. This became their symbol. He resigned in May 1979 and I was sorry to see him leave. We continued to work with the Mission. Ken spent sixteen years with SCM, helping it to become one of Australia's most successful and effective charities. It later became a national charity - Mission Australia.

Getting new business was essential. It was highly competitive. Because most clients already had an agency, they would have to be unhappy to move. I believed accounts are lost on poor service and won on creativity. It was easier if the client was new and wanted an agency. When I had been at JWT, I was on a committee with the CEO as chairman, to isolate, pitch and hopefully obtain new clients. JWT enjoyed the benefits of being the largest advertising agency in the world. The local Melbourne and Sydney offices were the second largest agencies in Australia.

Of course, you could only submit for clients not competitive to your current client. For example, JWT had the Benson and Hedges cigarette account. It couldn't take on a competitive company, like Philip Morris or Rothmans.

During my time working on new business at JWT, the New York office had produced a video on the changing trends in society and the implications for marketing and advertising. This was well produced, and we developed a program to invite prospective clients to view the video in the well-equipped theatre, with savouries and drinks to follow. We were successful in inviting companies but there were no immediate gains.

At TGA, we were successful in finding Christian clients, because our only competitor was Pilgrim. However, we needed to attract commercial clients with bigger budgets to enable the agency to grow. I had decided that one way was to publicise the agency in the trade magazines. We chose *B and T* (*Broadcasting and Television*) mentioned before, and *Advertising News*. We also published in the advertising sections of the *Australian Financial Review* and *The Australian* newspaper. Consequently, any new clients and staff appointments and even my trips overseas to visit existing clients' headquarters were publicised.

My other strategy was to write to prospective clients enclosing an agency brochure. I would follow up with a phone call to try to meet them and present our work and credentials. I didn't enjoy this. Again, the rejection rate was high.

To meet prospective clients, I joined the new members' committee of the Australian-American Chamber of Commerce and the Ad Club.

Undoubtedly one of the most exciting ways I met clients, was to join a unique two-day jaunt around Australia in a Qantas 747, The flight was for 278 VIPs each of whom paid $500 for the trip - equivalent to about $2,500 in today's money. Australia's richest man at the time, Lang Hancock, had written his first book, *Wake Up Australia*, in which he outlined the case for West Australian secession. And what could be a better way to launch it and celebrate his seventieth birthday than for his daughter, Gina, to plan this event. First, the initial response was slow, John Singleton, an old mate of Lang Hancock, had another mate write an advert, which resulted in over 300 enquiries.

Other problems developed. The main speaker from America, Dr Edward Teller - the father of the hydrogen bomb - had a heart attack and couldn't come. There was an outcry about women not being able to attend because of the lack of suitable accommodation at the overnight stop at North West Cape, Western Australia. This became a tent city with security guards everywhere. And to top it all, Lang Hancock caught a virus and couldn't attend. What else could go wrong for them?

Happily, from the moment we boarded the jet on 11 June 1979 to the next day, the *Wake Up Australia* trip was a huge success. The plane flew over gas and mineral plants in most states.

Surprisingly, with all my efforts, accounts would come via other ways. Personal contacts and networking were essential.

But I felt that I had to do my bit by being proactive. This new business need became a little obsessive. In meeting executives at a social function, I would ask: 'Where they were from? What work did they do?' If they were not in business, I would move on and work the room to find other prospects. I shudder now at this activity.

By the end of the 1970s, the agency was flourishing. I had achieved my goals.

'Pray big. Think big. Believe big.'
NORMAN VINCENT PEALE

CHAPTER 20

LIBERACE PLAYS - TGA SOARS

In 1975, TGA was appointed by Bruce Myers, CEO of Stedfast Enterprises, the money-making arm of Open-Air Ministries, a long-established interdenominational Christian organisation and the Australian distributor of US based Thomas Organs.

I had heard that Liberace, a famous American pianist, singer and actor was in Australia on another tour. He was at the peak of his career. Australian audiences, and especially older women, loved him. Liberace was a superstar. From the 1950s to the 1970s he was the highest paid entertainer in the world. He was flamboyant on and off the stage. He called himself 'Mr Showmanship'.

It would be a great coup if we could get Liberace to endorse Thomas Organs. I phoned Liberace's manager in Adelaide and we agreed to a $10,000 fee (an unbelievably tiny amount) for Liberace to appear in a TV commercial promoting Thomas Organs. This was an amazing opportunity. The client didn't have a big budget. We were their first advertising agent. We produced full page ads in the *Australian Women's Weekly* which raised the Thomas Organ profile and sold the product. The client could see the benefit of advertising. But this was a huge step, requiring an investment of over a quarter of a million dollars to produce the commercial and buy prime time spots on television. I remember phoning Bruce Myers on a Saturday morning and encouraging him to say, Yes. He said 'Yes', after consulting his Board.

So, we were going to make our first TV commercial with a top production crew. We had a few problems. First, Actors Equity wouldn't agree to Liberace doing the commercials in Australia. The only solution was for us to follow Liberace to America. Then the director, Allan Dickes, and cameraman, Peter James (who went onto film Driving Miss Daisy and scores of other films), flew to Las Vegas, only to find their hotel booking had vanished without trace because a Teamsters Union Convention had just about taken over the City.

The third drama happened when our creative director, Ross Meillon, went down with bronchitis while on the plane and was delayed 24 hours in Honolulu. Ross said, of writing the commercial, 'This is a traditional demonstration commercial with an older person (Liberace) showing a youngster the benefits of playing a Thomas organ because of its unique colour-glo keys'.

Using well-known personalities in advertising was very common. Ideally, in addition to being well known, they needed to relate to the product or service. Liberace fitted both requirements. The Unique Selling Proposition of the organ was the colour-glo keys, which would light up when the player touched the organ keys.

LIBERACE PLAYS - TGA SOARS

The commercial was shot in Liberace's Las Vegas home garage, complete with chandeliers. Ross said, 'It was big enough to qualify as an Australian television sound studio'.

The US head office of the Thomas Organ Company was stunned by the brashness of its Australian importers. They sent several top executives urgently from Chicago to Las Vegas to watch the filming, and then signed Liberace to a worldwide contract for Thomas Organ commercials. The only country that did not see Liberace at a Thomas Organ was America, because he was already contracted to a piano manufacturer.

On our return, the Thomas Organ commercial went to air with unbelievable results. People would walk into a store with over a thousand dollars in cash to buy a Thomas organ.

Once completed, Ross asked Liberace if he would do a short, five-second testimonial commercial for one of our other clients, the 'Christmas Bowl', annually run by the Australian Council of Churches. Liberace was only too happy to oblige. 'He was a wonderful, generous, man', Ross said. After several rehearsals and a lecture by Ross (a keen Methodist) on the aims and objectives of the appeal, Liberace played jolly Christmas tunes then, turning to the camera, spoke about those who's Christmas would be less than merry, and what Australians could do to help them. Television stations offered to show this commercial in peak viewing times, for free.

At TGA we thought we had a winner. But when the Christmas Bowl spot was shown to the Australian Council of Churches people, they knocked it back. 'Liberace's lifestyle doesn't agree with our values', they said. Ross was shattered. He explained, 'Liberace did the commercial for free. We've had one of the world's top entertainers endorse the Christmas Bowl and you knock it back!' *Time* magazine even wrote about their refusal and criticised their attitude.

The Liberace commercial put Stedfast Enterprises, Thomas Organs and Tom Glynn Advertising on the map.

'When the student is ready, the teacher will appear.'
TAO TE CHING

CHAPTER 21

DEALING WITH THE BLACK DOG

The saying 'Black Dog' was widely credited to Winston Churchill, in his battle with depression. Churchill wasn't the only well-known person to suffer from mental illness. Others were Van Gogh, Beethoven, Abraham Lincoln, Charles Dickens and Leo Tolstoy. It's said that a high proportion of creative people suffer from mental illness.

I had experienced depression in Singapore, exacerbated by the breakdown of my relationship with Lorna. This mood continued during my two years in London, where I would blame the weather, but it was actually depression, which was then undiagnosed. I didn't really understand what it was, but I had learnt to deal with it by toughing it out, etc. For more than twenty years, I kept my depression to myself, being embarrassed to talk about it.

I kept a journal for a time. On 26 March 1985, at forty-four years old, I wrote, 'Still depressed, seeking to get rid of it and enjoy the excitement of running TGA. However instead, I dread returning to the office on Monday mornings. It is no longer enjoyable. The agency has lost its excitement and challenge.'

I had always struggled with rejection. I thought I was in the wrong industry, because it was common to be rejected. However, I did largely learn to cope with it. The only role I knew was the ambitious, thrusting, young enthusiastic Tom Glynn who, for seven to eight years, devoted himself to building an agency, blocking out other interests, emotions and, most importantly, feelings.

I did want to get rid of the depression. It was worsened by a lack of confidence and certainty. At times I wanted to go back to where I'd been, but I couldn't. I searched for theological answers and help. Lynda and I attended monthly Jungian meetings.

I worried about money, and wondered how much was reality and how much was a reflection of my insecurity. I considered multiple options, including liquidating the business, merging with another agency, buying another agency, selling the agency or doing nothing at all.

I even wondered if changing my appearance - new hairstyle, a beard or glasses - would help. I was ready for a journey, but didn't know the destination. My metaphorical bags were packed but I didn't know where to go. I was stuck - a principal cause for people to seek therapy.

Change will only take place when the present unhappiness is given up for a new role. I wanted someone to tell me what I should do. Frank Grace had told me to go to Singapore - I went. John Adams asked me to join JWT - I did. I needed someone to tell me what to do.

DEALING WITH THE BLACK DOG

To be depressed is to enter a world no one wants to go. It's a world of frequently being sad, having no hope, no enthusiasm and thinking that it will all last forever. I was unmotivated. I would avoid going out with people. I would have lunch by myself. It would have been easier to have a broken leg instead of having depression - then family and friends would be able to see the injury. But depression is hidden, covered by a mask - in my case by extroversion and business success.

My underlying depression lifted with the excitement and energy of marrying Lynda in 1967 and again when I started TGA in 1974. These events temporarily kept the 'Black Dog' in its kennel.

But in January 1981 my father died suddenly of a burst aorta, caused, according to my doctor, by smoking. He had had no previous illnesses, and had rarely seen a doctor. Dad died after we'd had a happy, wonderful Christmas Day at our new home in Roseville. On the Saturday when he died, he was sitting on the veranda, at his home, with a cigarette and a glass of sherry, listening to the races on his transistor radio. Fortunately, my brother Bruce was there. Later I saw Dad's body at Lewisham Hospital. This was the first time I had seen a dead body, and it was the first death of a loved one.

This was a huge shock but, because of my fears and compulsion not to grieve, I kept going. To avoid any emotional pain on the night of his death, I ate a big chicken dinner. Friends and people at the office offered their sympathy, which I rejected. 'I'm okay', was my reply. I was strong and I would get over this loss. I didn't cry at his funeral.

When going through a mental illness, you sometimes believe getting away from the everyday will make you feel better. So in August 1982, Lynda and I, with Michael (10), Stephen (7) and Amanda (5), flew to Los Angeles, New York and England, hoping that a family trip would reduce my depression - it didn't!

There was more to come. Because of TGA's financial success, our accountant had recommended we invest large profits into a film scheme, which was legal at the time. But, during the Christmas/New Year holiday in 1982, John Howard, the then Treasurer, cancelled the 10AB Scheme and made the cancellation retrospective. I was hit with a huge back tax of a quarter of a million dollars. I was shattered, I said, 'It wasn't fair'. I was working hard to build a profitable business, employing staff, paying taxes and I'd acted on the recommendation of my trusted accountant. Not only did I have to pay the tax due, but I was also hit with the huge penalty as well.

With the double hit of the grief from the death of my Dad and the back-tax problem, the underlying depression I had had on and off over the years, seriously worsened. I fell into a deep depression.

But, I continued to put on the mask of a bright, happy, bushytailed ad-man, whilst inside I was suffering from this deep, depressive illness. I thought, wrongly, that I was in a mid-life crisis. Carl Jung wrote a lot about the mid-life crisis. For example, he wrote, 'But, we cannot live the afternoon of life according to the program of life's morning; for what in the morning was true will at evening have become a lie'.

At work, Ross Meillon, saw that I was depressed. He and his brother-in-law, a psychiatrist, were writing a book on the importance of genes in our lives. The brother-in-law believed that depression was caused by a lack of vitamins and food allergies. I had an appointment with him. He took hair samples and prescribed many vitamins, but they didn't work for me. I also saw another psychiatrist who was retired. He was not right for me either.

Then over the Australia Day long weekend in January 1985 I hit a crisis of feeling suicidal. Our family and a few other close friends had spent the three days together at a recreational venue at Elanora Heights, a twenty-minute drive from our homes on Sydney's North Shore. Nearby, were the beaches. Every day we swam and at night, we played board games after the children had gone to bed. It was a happy and carefree break before the Christmas/New Year holidays came to an end. Most people were due to return to work on the Tuesday.

However, it wasn't a happy time for me. I spent the available free time by myself, sitting in the sun, reading self-help books that I thought may lift my mood. No one, except Lynda, suspected that I was depressed.

Back at home on the Monday night I tossed and turned in bed. On awakening, I told Lynda I felt suicidal. Feeling desperate I phoned the Northside Psychiatric Clinic in St Leonards. Thankfully the message was passed to a nearby psychiatrist, who phoned me back and asked if I was suicidal. I answered 'Yes', and he then requested I come to see him at once. This was the beginning of a successful relationship of over thirteen years.

As the saying, goes: 'When the student is ready the teacher will appear'. I believe he was a blessing from God.

He quickly diagnosed that I was suffering from a genetic illness. It was in my DNA - Dad almost certainly suffered also, but he used to self-medicate by smoking and drinking. He also became addicted to gambling, which I later discovered was common with the highs of winning and the lows of losing.

His father, my grandfather, I am sure also experienced depression. When we occasionally visited him at Narrabeen, he would be sitting there, staring out at the Narrabeen Lakes. He didn't say very much and hardly noticed we were there.

The doctor prescribed anti-depressant medication, which relieved the symptoms. He was a great help and prevented me from acting on my suicidal thoughts. Such extreme action can become an option when people are suffering and not able to think straight. They can make unwise decisions, which can cause havoc to them and their families.

In the early days, I thought my depression was caused by my poor upbringing. Was I abused as a child? Was I cuddled enough? No, in my case it was clinical depression caused by a lack of serotonin in the brain.

I had long searched for meaning, to understand why I suffered from this depression. The discovery of a biological basis to my depression was a relief. At last, my psychiatrist had explained what caused the occurrence of my depressive symptoms.

I was fortunate, that I had found a suitable psychiatrist after my crisis of feeling suicidal over the Australia Day long weekend in January 1985. Finding the right health professional, who understood and could treat my clinical depression, had not been easy. It had been vital for me to be able to establish a good trusting relationship with him.

> 'Suffering is a foghorn from God.'
> C. S. LEWIS

CHAPTER 22

LEARNING ABOUT DEPRESSION

Over the years I had tried everything to relieve the 'Black Dog'. I was impressed by the words of Dante, written in the late thirteenth century. 'Midway in the journey of life, I came to myself in a dark wood, for the straightway was lost.'

I had attended the weekly healing service at St Andrews Cathedral, Sydney. I had taken up learning to play the organ, thinking a creative endeavour would help me. I had started a Men's group at home. Here we had discussed important subjects with confidentiality and openness. I had read many books on the mid-life crisis, ranging from Gail Sheehy's ground-breaking book *Passages*, to theological books on the mid-life crisis and spirituality in the second phase of life.

Many Christians believe that mental illness, including depression, can be cured simply by reading the Bible and praying. Others would encourage depressives to 'pick themselves up'. They would ask, 'Why are you depressed? - you have (list of achievements, etc.)'. But I found that depression is real and requires professional treatment, which can include counselling and/or prescribed medication.

Thankfully, mental illness is now regarded as a legitimate condition, like diabetes or high blood pressure. It needs to be treated! For some twenty years, I had kept my depression to myself, being embarrassed to talk about it. Now, I had learned to talk about it to those interested, to help add to the awareness of and treatment of mental illness.

For a long time, I had confused my depression as being a mid-life crisis. Some people believe that unhappiness will be reduced by exterior things, looking outside oneself - finding a new job/career, a new relationship. Some seek to remain youthful by buying a Harley Davidson motor bike and/or wearing a gold bracelet, etc. But all these are counterfeit destinations, going nowhere, in the hope of reducing or removing the psychological pain.

We know that depression is actually an 'inner job' - looking inward to find more about oneself, to understand what causes different moods. 'The only journey is the one within', said Rainer Maria Rilke. Ask what needs to change. 'We had the experience but missed the meaning.'

Learning about oneself and looking inwards is not for everyone. I estimate that up to 20% of people in Western countries are interested in personal growth and the inner journey and spirituality. The remaining 80% are generally not reflective. They escape through the popularity and huge ratings of TV reality shows, sport, gambling, and can often turn to alcohol and drugs. I hope I'm wrong. If not, it's a poor and disturbing summary of our society. We look for pleasure not pain - we want to be happy.

But as Epictetus wisely said, 'It's never the things that happen to us which upset us, it's our view of these things'. I am pleased that Hugh Mackay has written on this subject. His latest book, *The Inner Self: the joy of discovering who we really are*, will likely sell thousands of copies and add insights to people seeking more understanding.

As said earlier, I thought my depression was caused by a mid-life crisis and I searched everywhere to get rid of it. In the 1980s, I attended a series of talks by Dr Anthony Kidman, father of Nicole Kidman, about Cognitive Behavioural Therapy (CBT). Modern CBT had gained popularity in the 1960s and, since then, it had been shown to be an effective treatment for a number of mental health conditions, including depression. CBT focuses on the interconnection between our thoughts, behaviour and feelings, and how they can interact to create a vicious cycle. By making changes to what and how we think, we can reverse that cycle and improve the way we feel. (I have also used Relational Emotive Behaviour Therapy over the years, and it has helped me as well.)

More recently, I found out more about CBT on the internet and downloaded details of CBT Steps, which I then used during my life. It took quite a bit of practice and time to have much effect, but gradually I found it to be quite helpful, assisting in dealing with my depression.

I used it particularly to deal with my rejection:
- **Activating Event**. I had put a lot of time and energy into a proposal to the Sydney Royal Easter Show. I

was really expecting to win this one - but it was not accepted - I was devastated.
- **Irrational Belief**. I had failed, I was hopeless, Why do I fail all the time?, I'll fail again next time, I won't be able to cope, etc.
- **Emotional and Behavioral Consequences**. I became angry/depressed/withdrawn, my work colleagues saw my response, were concerned and kept their distance. Similarly my family was worried about me and didn't know how to deal with me.
- **Dispute or Question my Irrational Beliefs**. My usual way of dealing with such a rejection was to tell myself 'so what? - this won't kill me'. So, having now identified my Irrational Beliefs I began to dispute them: it wasn't really failure - it was just a setback, I wasn't hopeless - I've often been successful, I don't actually 'fail all the time' and I may not fail next time. I have been able to cope in the past.
- **New Feeling or Behaviour**. I felt growing relief that the loss of the Sydney Royal Easter Show bid was not the end of the world, I calmed down, became more positive and started to think of new options.

However whilst CBT assisted to put my experiences in perspective, I was still suffering from clinical depression. My problem was a medical condition.

I had felt insecure partly because I had no knowledge of when and where depression would rise up and overwhelm me. I wanted 'control' - to feel that I could overcome those feelings - and this spread to control of other parts of my life. I had to admit I was a 'control freak'. It had been difficult for me to sit back and allow myself to 'feel' and include that part into my identity. I wanted to conquer and delete the depressive part of myself.

I learned that depression is broadly divided into two causes. Endogenous depression occurs without necessarily experiencing stress or trauma. In other words, it has no apparent outside cause. Instead it is primarily caused by genetic and/or biological factors. I had this biologically based depression. On the other hand, reactive or exogenous depression happens, caused by stressful or traumatic events taking place. My clinical depression was aggravated by such life events.

Huge advances have occurred with the awareness of depression since the 1980s. It is no longer a stigma. Depressive illness is quite common - about one in five people will have a depressive episode during their lives. More and more celebrities come out and speak about their mental illnesses.

My one regret is that I didn't seek professional help for over twenty years. For a time, I had thought that I was suffering a mid-life crisis that would eventually lift. How wrong I was! Now, if I am aware of a person with depression, I encourage them to check their symptoms online and, if necessary, seek help.

A good friend's son in his early thirties tragically committed suicide. He was mentally ill and working. But his tipping point was losing his job and being made redundant. My friend and his wife learned about the brain having two sides, the right side being more intuitive, emotional, and creative. The left side being associated more with logical analytical thinking. With severely depressed people, the right side of the brain grows, and dominates the left. The result is that the emotional side takes over, causing the sufferer to believe the only way out of their pain is to take their life. One emotion missing was hope.

Antidepressants may be prescribed. I tried a few. It was a challenge to find the right one. For many, antidepressants don't work. Sadly, this can also lead to suicide - numbers of which are still increasing every year in Australia.

For all people, family genetics plays a part in our development. I sought approval of my performance and understanding of my financial wellbeing, possibly stemming from my lack of security and low self esteem. Whilst I now know that depression was always there - it was the breakdown of the relationship in Singapore, the sudden loss of my Dad and the huge fine from the film scheme, that caused the onset of my deep depression - that then initiated my seeking help.

My therapist said my greatest challenge was to learn to accept depression as an unwelcome part of myself into my self-awareness. By doing so, and accepting my depth of feeling in depression, I resonated with all the distressing parts of my life as well as enjoying all the pleasures. I am now sympathetic to people suffering generally, but especially to people suffering with mental health issues.

'Inch by inch, it's a cinch.'
ROBERT H. SCHULLER

CHAPTER 23

KEEPING GOING

In the latter 1980's the agency continued, but I was still suffering from depression. I still had to run an agency with about a dozen people, which was stressful. I had to keep going and tough it out. I had to make sure we had enough income from clients to pay our bills, and to help get new clients to replace the ones who had left. I had to find new staff. I also had to maintain my life as a father and parent of three young children, and keep turning up at Church, meetings and social events.

The psychiatrist had correctly identified my clinical depression as endogenous (part of my DNA) and that I needed anti-depressant medication. He prescribed SRNI (serotonin-norepinephrine reuptake inhibitor) medication, to increase the correct dose of serotonin to my brain and thus reduce my depression. But not all people with depression require anti-depressant prescribed medication.

Regularly seeing the psychiatrist was a great help, as a sounding board to the challenges I faced. The agency won a number of new clients, including Viva/Traveland, Golden Press books, PBS (Permanent Building Association of Building

Societies) and a few others. But we had a bad experience with one of them - HomeWorld Exhibition Village of project homes. In our submission to win the account, we created the name, 'HomeWorld'. We were working with a group of builders who had their own money in the project, which particularly made them want the best for their investment. They rejected our first campaign but approved our second submission, and the commercial was shot. Some weren't happy and, without discussing it with us, they had another agency do the work. This rejection hit me hard. Not only did we lose the income, but all our efforts in pitching for the account came to a halt.

Before shooting the commercial, the builders had asked for the copyright to use the name HomeWorld. Trying to please the client (a weakness), I gave it to them for free use. Usually, a fee is paid to the agency for creating a brand name. HomeWorld is still being used today.

Apart from the fee-paying charities, Anglican Home Mission Society and Uniting World Mission, we worked with the Bible Society, Crystal Cathedral/Hour of Power and the Haggai Institute. I felt that I had made it. At forty-two years of age, I had a good thriving agency and apparent financial security. I liked to have control and to take charge, which reduced my anxiety.

Another fee-paying client, Wesley Central Mission, was added in 1988. Wesley is a large Christian welfare society with a Church in Pitt Street, Sydney. Wesley Mission was founded in 1815 by a Methodist minister, Rev Samuel Leigh. In 1958 Rev Sir Alan Walker, KB, OBE was appointed as Superintendent, where he started Lifeline in 1963. Realising that the Church needed a strong voice in the community, and with the benefit

KEEPING GOING

of worldwide experience behind him, Walker took advantage of the relatively new medium of television to spread the Christian Faith.

Rev Gordon Moyes succeeded Alan Walker in 1978 and he spent twenty-seven years as Superintendent. Like Walker, Moyes was a shaker and doer in Sydney. He continued a high profile on TV and established new ventures - A Christmas in Darling Harbour, Vision Valley Recreational Centre, financial counselling, and suicide prevention services.

TGA was invited to pitch for the Wesley Mission business. Up to then, their communication and fundraising had been done in-house. Wesley also asked Pilgrim, the well-known art studio, now evolved into an ad agency, to submit. Pilgrim's Creative Director, Graham Wade, was a superb artist and a friend. Their main growth came with World Vision. Although friends, we were competitive because we were the only two agencies handing Churches and charities.

Moyes and his team came to our offices and we presented a TV campaign and new logo design. The slogan was based on, 'Because there's so much more to do'. The logo in blue and green removed 'Central' and it became 'Wesley Mission'. We said, in years to come, the word 'Mission' could also be dropped.

'Love it', said Moyes (without consulting his colleagues). 'You have the account. Well done!' This appointment, with a monthly fee, lasted for five years, with TGA handling media and fundraising.

I enjoyed working with Wesley Mission. They were professional in everything they did. Our contacts were senior executives from large commercial business organisations, who had joined Wesley to help others. This became a trend. Many people, including politicians, are now attracted to charities to provide their experience and abilities to help others.

'Come to me, all you who are weary and burdened, and I will give you rest.'
MATTHEW 11:28 NIV

CHAPTER 24

TGA SOLD

I knew burnout was common and my depression was activated by rejection and potential loss of financial security. Why, then, go into advertising, where rejection is common? It was crazy! There was regular rejection by creative works, staff and clients. It was as if I was placed on Earth to learn the hard way.

I knew I couldn't go back but I had to find a new direction. I read, 'Change will only take place when the present unhappiness is given up for the new role'.

I knew I was stuck in limbo between heaven and hell, the old and the new. I was angry with the psychiatrist for not telling me what to do. He challenged me, 'What do you want?' I liked reading, ideas, current trends, media, culture and films.

I had three options for the future: to sell the agency, to take over another agency with existing accounts, or to merge with another agency.

I ran a few advertisements in the *Financial Review*, offering to buy an agency or to merge. I approached a few agencies that I respected. I was tired of running TGA. Doing the monthly invoices, chasing slow payers, appointing staff, and making sure clients were happy. This was in addition to attending to the needs of Lynda and the children. I dreaded returning to the office on Mondays. The magic was gone. But the magician was still on the stage!

After a lot of soul searching and praying, I decided to sell the agency. Finally, in May 1989, I sold TGA to Pemberton Advertising, and signed a two-and-a-half-year contract. We moved up five floors to join Pemberton Advertising. I would continue to handle the Anglican Home Mission Society, Baptist Community Services and Wesley Mission, as well as the other TGA clients. I also worked on any new Pemberton accounts.

I sold TGA at the right time. In 1990 a mini recession hit Australia, and we would have struggled keeping the agency going. My friend and Creative Director, Ross Meillon, had already left TGA. Pemberton was a good agency. Managing Director, Terry Carr, and Creative Director, John Ayliff, owned the agency. They had also just bought another agency for which all the paperwork had been done. By selling, I removed the hassles of running my own agency, which helped to manage my depression. And more importantly, I didn't mind going to work on a Monday morning.

In 1993 my contract with Pemberton's finished, and I faced another challenge. At age fifty, do I retire or continue to work on my own as a consultant with two monthly paying clients? I knew I was not yet ready for retirement. The agency name, Tom Glynn Advertising was owned by Pemberton's, so I created Tom Glynn & Associates, looked for another office to rent, and commenced a new phase and chapter of my life.

When a person is suffering from a mental illness, it is obvious that their loved ones and friends may be affected. How did Lynda and our children, Michael, Stephen and Amanda, cope? The children had no idea at the time. I kept the mask on. Lynda said when the children were young, she had seen that I had a need to be in control and get my own way - which I was doing at TGA. I was fortunate that she learned it was best on most occasions to agree with me, as it was important for her to keep the peace and harmony, and keep the family functioning well.

I had known many successful men whose children had gone off the rails. I tried to be home every night at six, I attended most of their school activities and watched them play sport (Michael criticised me for reading the paper while he was playing). We were able to send them to private schools - Barker and Roseville Colleges.

After the children had left school, Lynda returned to work. She started by doing a 'Working with Older People' course at TAFE and attending courses run by the Diversional Therapy Association, to become a Recreational Activities Officer in Aged Care Facilities. She joined Turramurra House aged care facility, where she worked for twelve years, enjoying helping the elderly to maintain meaningful lives for themselves and continue to have sociable interaction with others.

I joked that Lynda would be qualified to look after me in my old age. But for now, I had new clients and challenges.

'It takes guts to get out of the ruts.'
ROBERT H. SCHULLER

CHAPTER 25

ON MY OWN

In 1994 Tom Glynn & Associates (which became the new TGA) was appointed by Baptist Community Care, another monthly fee-paying client. We produced their quarterly publication, *Trust*, wrote and produced their leaflets and fundraising materials, and designed a new logo, BCS.

Other Christian clients were CMS (Church Missionary Society) and, in 1995, Churches of Christ *Advance* publication, Samaritan's Purse, Pontifical Mission - and a new logo for their new identity, Christian Mission.

In the 1990s, New Age activities became popular. There was a yearly exhibition, 'Body, Mind and Soul' held at the Sydney Entertainment Centre. The Principal of Morling Baptist College, Rev Ross Clifford, had written a book with Philip Johnson on the New Age. They believed Christianity should also be there alongside other New Age exhibitors. They created a name, 'New Age Mission'. I became involved from 1996 with creating the themes and the production of the graphics for the stand, and printed materials.

Other activities included the NSW Council of Churches. This group comprised most of the denominations, but didn't include the Uniting Church, the Roman Catholics or the Pentecostal Charismatic groups. It was a highly conservative group dominated by the wealthy Sydney Anglican Diocese. The jewel in the Council of Churches' crown was radio station 2CH, which was started in 1932 - the 'CH' stood for Churches.

I became the Board member for Churches of Christ. The Council had arranged for Sunday broadcasts on 2CH to be given over to Churches and Christian groups. The weekday programs were gentle, middle of the road music. Bob Rogers was the morning host. Ad-man John Singleton bought the station in 1994 and, to his credit, maintained the Christian presence. It was sold in 2017 and again in 2020, and in late 2020 became SEN 1170 - 'Sydney's home of sport'. However, the traditional Sunday night Christian program is now hosted by a Christian sports personality. Called 'Spirit of Sport', the compere is currently Jason Stevens.

Being the Churches of Christ board member, I also became an Executive of the Council's Broadcasting Committee. As fewer people were Church attendees, and with increasing secularisation, it was hard for the NSW Council of Churches voice to be heard in the media. Most of the Committee members were retired. Sydney Anglicans were the largest contributors financially, and had the most members, most of whom were younger and tended to dominate the Council.

As Tom Glynn & Associates (TGA), I didn't want to work from home. I enjoyed having people around me. So I sought friends who ran advertising agencies and who may have had room for me to move in, pay a small rent and use their facilities. I was lucky to have worked with three such agencies. Sadly, all have now ceased to exist, including Pemberton's. Advertising is a hard, ruthless business. I felt like I was the 'Angel (or Agent) of Death' and, not wanting to inflict this on others, I eventually decided it was best to work from home in Roseville.

I have been well looked after by friends in the advertising world. Frank Grace was a mentor. John Adams found me a job at J. Walter Thompson. Terry Carr bought Tom Glynn Advertising. Other friends gave me a desk. I believed it was important in business to network - to meet other people. Most jobs are not advertised, but positions are filled by people known within the specific industry.

Then, a crisis! The Anglican Home Mission Society's new CEO sacked TGA and appointed Pilgrim. This was common practice - a new CEO or Marketing Director is appointed and changes the advertising agency. When I started work, client and agency relationships were strong. A Managing Director on the client side and the ad agency CEO would be involved in the work. TGA had serviced the Anglican Home Mission Society for twenty-three years, a record time. And then, to make matters worse, within a month BCS decided to go in-house, and cancelled our contract. So, my security blanket of two fee-paying monthly accounts was gone.

Again, I felt low. At fifty-six years of age, had my time come to retire?

My brother, Bruce, had retired at fifty-eight years from McCann's Advertising Agency, to live in his Pearl Beach home with his partner, a generous man loved by our family, Ken Watts. Ken died from throat cancer in 1996 - he was 64 years of age,

What was to be the next chapter of my life? Could I re-invent myself? I was telling clients and friends that you should review your operation and your life every three years because of the rapid and unrelenting changes in society. I needed to follow my own advice, and to re-invent myself - and find a new challenge.

'Bloom where you are planted.'
ST FRANCIS DE SALES

CHAPTER 26

CHURCH GYPSIES

Since our return to Sydney in 1968, and living on the North Shore of Sydney, Lynda and I were involved in North Sydney Baptist Church for a year before moving to a smaller Church, East Lindfield Baptist Church. Built in 1969, this Church attracted young families and we soon became active members. I became an Elder, Lynda taught Sunday School and helped run the Playgroup. Lynda was baptised there by Rev Norris Brook.

Our children Michael, Stephen and Amanda attended Sunday School. They attended Boys' Brigade and Girls' Brigade. The boys were amazed when they were older that not every child was a Church goer. It was a happy time.

In 1988, after two and a half years at the Church, the minister, Rev Phil Hazleton left. The younger members were shattered. Phil had been a breath of fresh air, teaching contemporary theology and ways to know yourself and others better.

Phil was training to be a psychologist and possibly, despite this, his insight drove him to resign and move on. The 'old brigade' filled the void, and we grieved Phil's move and decided to leave. For a while, we took time out and then, realising that the children needed a Church community, we joined Roseville Uniting Church for about two years. It was a thriving Church within walking distance from our home. I became involved in producing fundraising materials for a major extension.

Norris Brook, had become a friend and had moved to be an Associate Minister at Northside Community Church, at Crows Nest. This was a Church of Christ and its senior minister, Jay Bacik, was charismatic and effective in combining three small, struggling Churches, Mosman, North Sydney and Lane Cove. He had a Sunday night open line session on Radio 2CH and had daily radio commercials, which Jay and I printed in a book. During this time, divorce rates were growing. This impacted Christian couples, and Jay Bacik ministered to a large group of divorced men and women through a course called, 'Starting Over'.

I had known Jay for several years. We would have lunch and he would ask me for ideas and slogans. With the encouragement of Norris, we started attending Northside in 1991.

I was an appointed an Elder and in September 1991, the Church asked me to join the staff. I prayed about it and felt it wasn't the right fit. Instead, I contributed to the promotion of the Church as it grew. I and another person ran several twelve-week courses based on M. Scott Peck's best-selling book, *The Road Less Travelled*. In late 1991, M. Scott Peck visited Sydney and we arranged for Jay Bacik to compere the meetings - a coup! We distributed leaflets at the seminars, which advertised a series of sermons Jay would preach over the following five Sundays at Northside.

I was familiar with Peck's work after attending a course in the 1980s, when personal growth courses were extremely popular. Lynda and I did courses run by the Family Life Movement called, 'Free to Live, Free to Love' and courses on Myers Briggs, Enneagram, and Jungian archetypes. For some unknown reason, personal growth courses have gone out of fashion today. Lynda and I enjoyed the insights and were helped by attending the courses to understand ourselves.

One course I attended and was sad that it didn't continue in Sydney was based on M. Scott Peck's book, *The Different Drum. Community making and Peace*. Peck said there is a yearning in the heart for peace. Because of the wounds and rejections we have received in past relationships, we are frightened by the risks. In our fear, we discount the dream of authentic community as merely visionary. But there are rules by which we can come back together and the old wounds can be healed. Peck concludes, 'The purpose of Community Building is to teach these rules - to make hope real again - and to make the vision actually manifest in a world which has almost forgotten the glory of what it means to be human'.

I did the Community Building Workshop. It was held over two days. Some fifty people were with me. We sat in a circle and were encouraged only to speak when we had something important and relevant to say. There were four stages we had to experience. The first stage was called 'Pseudo Community'. This is what we do every day - being pleasant to one another, the superficial surface stuff with no depth-avoiding difficult issues. Trust is shallow. We want to belong. After about an hour or more, we enter stage two, 'Chaos', where individuals try to manage the differences that begin in the group - causing a lack of effective listening among members, the formation of cliques, efforts to solve each other's problems, unrealistic expectations and judgements both of oneself and of the others. Over a long time, people begin to grow weary of avoiding uncomfortable undercurrents and begin to speak out. Others do so, also. This is a sort of realism. But in confrontation we lack the trust that is needed for members to speak very personally. This is true Chaos.

After lunch participants entered the third stage, 'Emptiness'. Here, tired of trying to fix others, we slowly let go of the barriers that have been keeping members from being fully present. We resent something someone has said or done. Some tried to control the group. Fight or flight - or the third way - into and through Emptiness. This stage was not pleasant.

On the next day, people moved to the fourth stage, 'Community'. This is where we respect individual differences: there is a depth of listening, an unusual level of group safety, the possibility of spiritual and emotional healing, shared leadership, softened (respectful) conflict, effective group decision making, a sense of belonging, a greater awareness of what stage the group is in and what is needed to move it forward. To me, it was a powerful seminar and would be helpful for unions and management, governments, Churches, voluntary groups and other groups experiencing conflict.

Apart from an involvement with Scott Peck, Jay had a remarkably close connection with Robert Schuller, the minister of the mega Church Crystal Cathedral in Orange County, California. Schuller preached 'Possibility Thinking' based on his mentor, Dr Norman Vincent Peale's best-selling book *The*

Power of Positive Thinking. Schuller had preached at Northside Community Church.

Schuller's TV program *The Hour of Power* was screened in Australia to acceptable ratings for a religious program. The Crystal Cathedral ran an annual Church Leaders' seminar in January. A few us from Northside flew to Los Angeles and were treated to three days of stimulating speakers. We returned, thinking how Northside could implement these life and Faith affirming insights. Schuller wrote scores of books.

Tom Glynn & Associates had worked with the *The Hour of Power* local representative. He had a personal project that he wanted to launch in Australia, so he came into our office where he outlined the project to a few of us. After he had finished, we said 'it wasn't too bad'. Speaking to him later, he thought the comment was negative, a failure. 'No', I replied, 'when Australians say, "not too bad" we mean it's good'. This demonstrated a cultural difference between Americans and Australians.

I met Robert Schuller in the home of his Australian personal assistant on the Crystal Cathedral campus. He was tall and distinctive looking, as seen on his TV shows.

Dr Schuller founded the Crystal Cathedral Church in 1955, and by the 1980s it was drawing more than 10,000 worshippers each week. He started the *The Hour of Power* in 1970. On retiring in 2006, his son Robert A. Schuller took over the programme. However he resigned in 2008 after a falling out with his father. The younger Schuller started his own Church. Family tensions increased. People left. Donations plummeted. Finally, the Church became bankrupt, owing US$57.5 million. It was bought by the Catholic Diocese of Orange County.

Sadly, other well-known Church leaders have fallen because their egos grew out of control. Sexual and financial abuse, family feuds are the main reasons for their decline. Jesus would weep.

My other activities at Northside included filming Phil Johnson's talks on New Age Mission. Despite not being well filmed (and having to delete shots of the carpet), it was sold nationally via a mail out to Australian Churches. It was successful and we covered the costs.

Tim Foot was Northside's musical director and a talented author. He and an associate minister co-authored several short plays that could be used by Churches, called *Drama to Go*. Again, Tom Glynn & Associates promoted this to Churches, and the DVD was also a success.

'On the right path, the limping foot recovers strength and does not collapse.'

HEBREWS 12:13 J. B. PHILLIPS

CHAPTER 27

ANOTHER OPPORTUNITY

Our third fee paying client, Wesley Mission, also stopped in 1995. With the loss of three fee-paying clients, I needed to reinvent myself, and I saw a gap in the publishing market. I created a concept called, 'Which…' The first project was, 'Which Australian Advertising Agency?' Most ad agencies were foreign owned, but a few were still Australian owned.

A 'dummy' of the format was done and posted to the prospects. The concept was that Australian owned ad agencies would take space to promote themselves in the A5 publication, which would be inserted in a well-respected business magazine, *BRW - Business Review Weekly*. A few agencies booked space but not enough to make the concept viable.

I then moved to the Christian market, which I knew well. The first one was 'Which Christian Rest and Recreation Centres?' This was directed to Churches and schools looking for a venue for a weekend or a conference. Initially it was successful, with a handful of bookings, but the CEO of the Christian Venues Association quashed it. He argued that he was planning a guide and didn't want a competitor. Another failure, but I kept going.

Next, 'Which Christian Mission?' - directed to Churches in NSW which were looking for a Mission to support. Again, packs containing a 'dummy' of the format, a letter with costs, distribution details and reply information, were posted to the Mission organisations, inviting them to advertise and promote their Mission to Churches and individuals. Like all direct mail projects, it had to be followed up by a phone call.

Knowing I hated being rejected and I knew I wasn't the only person to feel this way. I had to overcome my reluctance to use 'the black snake' (an old insurance industry term for the telephone, which used to be black). I overcame this by placing a bank note marked $1,000 on my computer, knowing that I would make a sale with one-in-ten calls. So, with ten calls I would make $1,000. The other nine rejections didn't worry me. But, the calls were successful and we had enough bookings to publish the first edition.

It worked! The first issue we published was supported by a website: *www.whichchristian.org.au*. Other titles followed, 'Which Christian College?' and 'Which Christian School?' (Including both private and Church-based schools.) Two failures were 'Which Christian Resource?' and 'Which Cause to Support?', which were meant to take advantage of cause related marketing, influencing companies to support charities. My slogan was - 'doing good, is good for business'.

The 'Which Christian' publications and website continued, with websites replacing print, until, after fifteen years, when I finally retired and handed the business over to Rod Heard, who was the artist.

ANOTHER OPPORTUNITY

It was a challenge to distribute the publications. I joined forces with a Christian video supplier and mailed copies to thousands of Churches in Australia. These publications opened the door to establish relationships with most Missions, Christian schools, and Colleges.

One advertiser became another fee-paying client. Compassion was a competitor to World Vision. What do you do when your competitor, the largest child sponsorship charity, World Vision, spends thousands of dollars on advertising? Compassion created a 'niche' market by their strategy to gain sponsorships directly from Congregations in Churches. Compassion had State representatives who would visit the Churches, present the Compassion story, and gain sponsorships.

Based in Newcastle, Compassion Australia was started by Laurie and Olive McGowen in their Newcastle home. Laurie McGowan was a saintly man. We were sponsors and, on a trip north, Lynda and I visited them to say how we were impressed with their ministry. At the same time, entertainer Cliff Richard, another sponsor, was on tour in Australia. We began talking about the challenge for Compassion to gain more sponsors. We decided to test if an advert in secular newspapers would work.

I recommended we run advertisements with Cliff endorsing Compassion in the TV/Entertainment section of the *Sydney Morning Herald*. The ads ran and were noted by existing and new sponsors. Compassion had an artist on staff, but no one to plan and implement their promotion. So, in February 1998, TGA was appointed, again with a monthly fee.

To position Compassion against the big budgets of World Vision, we created the slogan, 'Compassion That's Completely

Christian', for a number of years before their American office introduced, 'Releasing Children from Poverty in Jesus' Name'. The ideal slogan is three to five words.

With declining Church attendance and finding it harder for Church presentation, Darlene Zschech, singer and songwriter for Hillsong Church, became involved, endorsed the ministry, and then she travelled to Thailand to see the work being done. We enjoyed a wonderful association with Compassion for years, despite a weekly drive from Sydney to Newcastle. Lynda and I still sponsor a child.

We were placing Compassion full page advertisements in two Christian publications, *Christian Woman* and *Alive*. Both had been successful over the years, but circulation and advertising income was fading. TGA became their sales agents to attract advertisers, which was successful, but it wasn't enough. Matt Danswan of Initiate Media bought both magazines. Sadly, the printed copies no longer exist. Another opportunity to work with Christian organisations, Hope Health Care (now part of Hammond Care) came on board in 1997.

In speaking at a Fundraising Conference, in 2004, I met Martyn Teulan. He introduced us to the CEO of the Pontifical Mission Society, who was looking to rebrand the Catholic Mission. We were happy to work with Catholic organisations but rejected The Church of Jesus Christ and Latter-Day Saints (the Mormons) when they asked us to plan and spend their substantial TV media budget. Their theology was too far removed from our own.

Following Catholic Mission, Martyn moved to a new start-up venture, called 'Church Resources' in 2001.

ANOTHER OPPORTUNITY

Father Michael Kelly SJ, a Jesuit, was an entrepreneurial parish priest who created a business model where a range of products and services, bought at bulk rates, were offered to Catholic Churches and organisations. Father Kelly founded 'Jesuit Publications' and launched 'Eureka Street'. This was a ground floor opportunity, where TGA used the slogan, 'Saving Plus' on promotional materials. It is still operating today under a new name.

Mission Statements became popular in the 1980s among businesses and even Churches. It became a fad - every group had to have one. I would work with our clients to help them write a distinctive and effective Mission Statement. Not to be left out, I wrote one for Tom Glynn & Associates, which read:

> *'TGA provides outstanding, highly-effective, marketing strategies and creative materials, which fulfil their client's marketing goals. We do this by listening to the client, their customers, reviewing their goals, their market and competitors.*
>
> *TGA only works with clients whom they value and believe in. TGA does this by offering to make a difference with the promise 'results not just promises'.*

Was this an ego trip? I hope not. I believed every word.

> 'Creativity is the process that gives life to a new product.'
> JAMES TAYLOR

CHAPTER 28

FAME - A NEW CONCEPT

From the end of 1999 to 2006 I developed a new service to Christian Missions called FAME, which stood for Fundraising, Audit and Marketing Evaluation. In accordance with my personal mission statement from in my twenties, I wanted to help Christian causes to be more efficient in their fundraising and marketing activities. I was impressed by a saying from Fyodor Dostoyevsky, 'The mystery of human existence lies not in just staying alive but in finding something to live for'. I believed I was in this category.

What began back with the Anglican Home Mission Society and the Scripture Union in 1973, we were now implementing fundraising for them, and other organisations. The 'Which' publications and website were going well. The FAME initiative was based on answering five simple but basic questions:

1) WHERE ARE WE NOW? Where does your organisation stand now in the market and minds of your target audience?

2) WHY ARE WE THERE? What factors have contributed to your strengths and weaknesses?

3) **WHERE COULD WE BE?** What realistically could be the position of your organisation in the future?
4) **HOW COULD WE GET THERE?** What changes and what elements in the fundraising, marketing, communication mix, could help achieve it?
5) **ARE WE GETTING THERE?** Is the plan achieving its objective and are the total strategies working?

The fee for this study was not large and came with a proviso - unless the fee can be achieved by new funds paying for it, we would refund the fee.

Fortunately, all projects were successful, and no refunds were given. I spent a day or two with the organisations, speaking to their staff, their donors and board members. Most projects included concepts for promotional materials, including fundraising concepts. I was helped by a freelance copywriter and an art director.

The best way to get business is from a referral from a satisfied client. This principle has helped us over the years and was included in all our new business proposals. We were fortunate in implementing FAME for these organisations:

Christian Woman Magazine. New subscribers and increasing advertising. We continued selling advertising space.

Hope Healthcare. Previously known as Baptist Inner-City Mission.

Samaritan's Purse. Created by Billy Graham's son Franklin.

Compassion Child Sponsorship. Resulted in an ongoing monthly fee.

Campus Crusade for Christ. We recommended a name change as 'Crusade' was a dated concept and Campus, an American word, was limiting their new initiatives. They have since developed a new name, Power to Change. We also helped them to distribute the Jesus Film project, which has been seen by many thousands.

Church of Christ Theological College. Name changed to ACOM - the Australian College of Ministries.

Mission Without Borders. A range of new creative materials for a Mission serving in Eastern Europe.

Queensland Baptist Union. Methods to increase Church giving and provide their various departments with a common style. Changed the name of their publication from Queensland Baptist to QB.

The Samaritans. Newcastle based charity. Slogan - 'Doing Good Locally'.

'I'd rather attempt to do something great and fail than attempt to do nothing and succeed.'
ROBERT H. SCHULLER

CHAPTER 29

YOU CAN'T WIN THEM ALL

In another effort to re-invent myself in 1998, I saw an opportunity to join George Patterson Advertising Agency, heading up a new division to service their large number of pro-bono charity clients. George Patterson was then the largest advertising agency in Australia, and one of the oldest. It served a large range of top advertisers.

I had worked for the London branch, Hobson Bates & Partners, and had met Bruce Jarrett, their Creative Director at the World Advertising Conference. I also knew Alex Hammill, who was the CEO. Alex and I had met at the School of Applied Advertising and at Jackson Wain where, like me, he was a junior account executive.

My plan was simple. Because of George Patterson's size, many well-known charities were delighted when 'Patts' did their promotion. I saw an opportunity not only to serve these charities but to add more and charge a fee for doing so.

At the same time, Cause Related Marketing (CRM) had arrived in Australia. CRM was based on the evidence that a company partnering with a charity would increase their sales.

I had started a business called 'Cause Communications' and wrote an article about it, which was published in *The Australian*.

An advertisement with the same heading, with a halo at the top of a grocery pack, included my slogan - 'Doing good, is good for business'. At Patterson's, doing advertisements for charities would take up valuable time by creative teams, when they could more profitably use their time doing ads for large advertisers. My unit would do the ads for the charities and service them.

I developed a well-prepared document, typed by my son Stephen, and personally presented to Alex Hammill in his palatial office in North Sydney. Alex was impressed. The objectives, strategies, implementation, and profits were set out clearly and, I thought, convincingly. The document was passed to the Managing Director, who also thought it was sound.

Unfortunately, another senior executive wasn't impressed, and the project was dropped.

Son Stephen was encouraging, 'Dad, it was a great document, and they should have bought it'. Another rejection!

A decade later and 'Patts' fortunes declined. It was taken over by a group of financers and later merged with Young and Rubicam. George Patterson is no longer - another agency gone. Why do companies and people who reject me fail? Does someone up there like me?

> 'To live is to change and to be perfect
> is to be changed often.'
> **CARDINAL JOHN HENRY NEWMAN**

CHAPTER 30

MY TWO SELVES

As someone who struggles with rejection and insecurity, it may seem odd that I went into advertising, where rejection was common. Clients would reject creativity, ask for staff to be removed from their account, and the biggest rejection was to move their business elsewhere.

With any mental health problem, it's vital to find a good therapist, the right medication and dosage. It took me three times to find the right therapist, and several types of anti-depressants and varying dosages to find the one right for me. Another thing that helped me was a strong need to be well. I would do anything, I told my psychiatrist, I would even walk down Martin Place naked, to get rid of the 'Black Dog'. A Bible verse helped me tremendously:

'On the right path, the limping foot recovers strength and does not collapse.' Hebrews 12:13, J. B. Phillips. (He suffered from depression. In addition to his New Testament translation, he wrote *The Wounded Healer*.)

I honestly believed I was on the right path. And during this period of struggle, I was also trying to move from the 'False

Self' to the 'True Self'. This concept was introduced in 1960 by psychoanalyst Donald Winnicott. He used True Self to describe a sense of self based or spontaneous, authentic experience and a feeling of being alive, as having a real self.

The False Self, by contrast, Winnicott saw as a defensive façade, which could leave people feeling dead and empty, merely appearing to be real.

For most of my career, I maintained a False Self. I was enthusiastic, eager to please and go the extra mile, and prepared to exceed clients' expectations. But many working people have a False Self, especially in sales, marketing and advertising. Wanting to please, impress others, we put on the mask. The challenge is to recognise this and to move from a False Self to the True Self.

Now I believe I've moved from a False Self to a 'Partial Self', and my True Self is more my 'Whole Self'. I don't need to explain, to overcome, to control either myself or the world around me. The challenge is to know who I am and learn to value not only the 'good bits', but also the 'bad bits' and learn how to make use of them.

Ted Scott Swan writes, 'You cannot do anything to become your True Self. Rather, you must simply step out of the way of your True Self. Stop restricting it. All that must happen for something real to surface, is for the false to be taken away. But, don't worry, the only things you can lose, are meant to be lost.'

Richard Rohr says the Christian journey involves God pushing us forward to a mature True Self. He writes, 'Normally the way God pushes us is by disillusioning us with the present mode. Until the present falls apart, we will never look for something more. We will never discover what it is that really sustains us. That dreaded falling-apart experience is always suffering in some form. All of us hate suffering, yet all religions talk about it as necessary. It seems to be the price we pay for the death of the small (False) Self and the emergence of the True Self - when we finally come to terms with our true identity in God.'

Wise words, practicing silence, journaling, talking with a trusted friend, are my ways to grow spiritually. Irenaeus, a philosopher, and theologian in the second century said, 'The glory of God is the human person fully alive'.

Once, a client was sacked and came to my office distressed. He sat down and I saw his pain. I heard his rejection, anger, and frustration. I listened carefully, not giving advice. Years later, we met up again and he thanked me for our time together and said how he saw a different side of me - not the pushy extrovert, but a person who was really concerned about him.

> 'There is no gain without pain.'
> BENJAMIN FRANKLIN

CHAPTER 31

PLUSES AND MINUSES

I was enjoying a coffee with a group of friends recently when one confessed that he would lie awake at night thinking about his regrets. I encouraged him to list them later, and alongside them write the good things. He said the good things would always win, ten times over.

Like all people I, too, have regrets. I would have liked to have gone to a better school, not to have cheated in my final year exams and to have gone to University. More importantly I wish I had understood my depression back to my time in Singapore. I also wish I had not wasted five years in my forties, thinking I was in a mid-life crisis, instead of recognising and seeking help for my depression. I would like to have been stronger in not caving in to clients demanding lower fees, and handing over the copyright for a new business (HomeWorld) to a client who then sacked TGA.

There have been some disappointments with friends. One industry friend, whom I had known for over twenty years and regarded as a mentor, had, along with me, been introduced to a new kitchen manufacturer who became our client. My friend was reluctant to call on him, but I insisted. We decided he would do the creative work, I would handle the media placement, and we would split the income fifty/fifty. The advertising was a great success. However, after many months, my friend who was closer to the client than I was, phoned to say TGA was no longer involved and that he would handle the account by himself. I was shattered by his action. Sadly, we never spoke again.

As a principle, perhaps caused by Scottish blood, I have always avoided debt, except for a home mortgage. And, as my friend with regrets, I too have enjoyed many successes. TGA had very few bad debts (apart from the back-tax drama) - in fact, never more than $10,000 in all. However, there could have been a big financial loss, with a client who was late in paying and could have gone into liquidation, owing TGA over $50,000. The client approached several companies and agreed to include them in full-page advertisements under a general banner with a leading Sydney radio personality to add his endorsement. This was powerful because of the radio identity's fame.

We couldn't get insurance cover for this client if he couldn't pay his bills. Therefore, we arranged for the client to pay TGA before the ads appeared. However he was late in paying us. Despite many phone calls, there was no response or cheques.

Luck was on our side. The radio personality was a client of our long-time accountant. In conversation, the accountant said to the radio personality that TGA was a good client and agency, and was going places. The personality mentioned TGA to his client, who replied he was using us for placing the ads in the media. Being aware that any negative comment about slow payment could jeopardise their relationship, the full amount was paid, and we returned to payment up front when the advertising space was booked.

Being a success in any form of life requires ambition, planning, insight, perseverance and luck. I was a reader of business and management books, including Peter Drucker (his book *The Effective Executive*, is still relevant today), Charles Handy and Edward D. Bono. I enjoyed reading books on advertising. David Ogilvy wrote two: *Confessions of an Advertising Man* and *Ogilvy on Advertising*. I also enjoyed *My Life in Advertising* by Claude C. Hopkins, *From Those Wonderful Folk Who Gave You Pearl Harbour*, by Jerry Della Femina, and *Positioning the Battle for Your Mind*, by Al Ries and Jack Trout.

I used Maslow's Hierarchy of Needs in our work. I conducted courses based on M. Scott Peck's *The Road Less Travelled* and Steven R. Covey's *Seven Habits of Highly Effective People*. I read *Time* magazine, business and fundraising journals.

I would quote statements to TGA staff. 'Everyone wants to be loved', 'Always deliver more than expected', 'Add the Wow factor' - and many more. My advertising philosophy was 'Tell me quick and tell me true. Less of how you came to be. More of what you can do for me.' In other words, what is in it for the consumer? I tried to let any muddy waters clear before deciding. And I would sleep on a problem and pray. In contacting companies, I would write to the CEO, not phone or email. In jest, I would say, 'most people are aiming for mediocrity and missing'.

My principles of effective advertising haven't changed over the years. The techniques and delivery of the message have. In 1974, I gave a talk at a Marketing Seminar for Religious Communicators under the heading, 'You have to remove your "rose-tinted glasses" before you plan a successful campaign'. I said, 'In this communication-overloaded society, the communication psychologists propose that we have learned to "rank" or "grade" products and services that demand our attention. What this means is, that given a product category, an average person will only recall about seven products within that category - the seven that have been the most effectively communicated or advertised.' A current example is the internationally best selling Mexican beer, Corona. With the Coronavirus (COVID19), their brand recognition will likely soar. I continued, 'There were three principles of effective communication. First: Know your product/service intimately. You should know as much as possible about your own activity - your strengths and weaknesses related to the competition. Use research to fill in the gaps and to back up your judgement. Second: Know your prospective market. Whatever you must sell, there's a specific market you want to sell to. No one can be all things to all people. Select the most profitable group to influence, and learn as much as you can about them. Third: Plan your approach and strategy, and keep planning. Great communication/advertising comes from great ideas. Such ideas can come in the shower or on the golf course, but are only likely to come consistently within the context of a defined planning system.'

In working with Churches, I quoted James W. Fowler, author of *Stages of Faith*, where he sought to develop the idea of a developmental process in human faith. He states Stage 0: as Primal Faith, Stage 1: Intuitive-Reflective Faith, Stage 2: Mythic-Literal Faith, Stage 3: Synthetic-Conventional Faith, Stage 4: Individuated-Reflective Faith. It sounds complex, but helpfully explains why some Christians object to changing anything in the Church. Well worth a read.

Another insight was relevant to Churches wishing to do what they had always done. Albert Einstein is popularly credited with the saying, 'Insanity is doing the same thing over and over again and expecting different results'. I also repeated the statement from Gary Hamel, an American management consultant, 'On "holding" or "folding" a Church activity'.

Dakota tribal wisdom says that when you discover you're on a dead horse, the best strategy is to dismount. Of course, there are other strategies. You can change riders. You can get a committee to study the dead horse. You can benchmark how other companies (groups) ride dead horses. You can declare it's cheaper to feed a dead horse. You can harness several dead horses together. But after you've tried all these things, you're still going to have to dismount.

'The glory of God is man fully alive.'
SAINT IRENAEUS

CHAPTER 32

MAN ALIVE

Since my thirties, I have been involved and interested in meeting men. I'd better emphasise that that's not about my sexual orientation. I have been involved with Men's groups, which developed in the 1960s and 1970s in western cultures, often in response to the Women's Movement and feminism. American authors saw the trend and wrote best-selling books, which included *Ironman John* by Robert Bly, *Fire in the Belly* by Sam Keen and *The Wildman's Journey* by Richard Rohr.

I think my interest with Men's groups could have been influenced by my need to find male mentors because of Dad's inadequate parenting. And also to find a peer group of men with their own businesses - I wanted to learn how they were coping. I was also disappointed to see older men in the Churches not growing in wisdom and understanding of a more mature Faith. Why was this so? I asked. The Bible talks about personal growth. It uses the word sanctification. This Greek word means 'holiness' or in my understanding 'wholeness'.

My observation of men who were struggling to overcome their problems and to become more mature was the catalyst for me to write a paper called *The Glory of God is Man Fully Alive*. With a sub caption, *The Problem: Australian Men, an Endangered Species*. Written almost thirty years ago, the challenges are still with us today and include - the rise and generally accepted Women's Movement and feminism, which impacted some men's roles in the family and community. Some men particularly were affected by marriage breakdown. Today most divorces are initiated by women. Gender inequality with higher household/emotional labour placed on women in marriages, and control and abuse from men could be a factor. An American survey showed that divorced women are typically happier after ending their marriages. Another subject in the paper was about men struggling with career and employment. Job security no longer existed. This is even more frightening now from the impact of the COVID19 pandemic.

My final point from my paper was that men were an endangered species who died younger than women. We self-destruct through alcohol, smoking, drugs, poor diet, compulsive behaviour, anger and depression. Men's suicide rates are higher than women's. Men make up 75% of suicides: the highest proportion is in the age range of 45 to 49. Men find it harder to show or express their feelings. Women generally have a network of friends, which encourages sharing and expressing of their feelings.

The challenge for men, I wrote, was to grow into Christian maturity. We would model Men's groups on Jesus, who founded a small group of twelve disciples who changed the world. We may not change the world but can work in our 'sand box', a metaphor for where we live and work.

I have been involved with Men's groups for many years. I confess I'm a Men's group 'groupie'. All groups share basic principles of confidentiality, honesty, vulnerability, cooperation, but not competition - which can be hard for some men. We avoid giving advice and 'rescuing' a man from his struggles, and we try to be a True Self not a False Self. Total confidentiality is essential. Anything said in the group stays in the group. There is an open door. Men can come and go as they wish.

My first group was in our home at Roseville. It ran for about four years. One of the participants took it over and it has run now for over twenty-five years. I attended a breakfast group with men who were running their own businesses. I attended weekend conferences with big numbers of men, which had speakers giving quick fixes and simplistic solutions like the need for Faith, to read the Bible and pray.

But possibly the most interesting Men's group was sponsored by 'The Fellowship' in Washington, USA, which ran the Presidential Prayer Breakfast (now called the National Prayer Breakfast) every year. They sent a keen and enthusiastic man and his family to Sydney to network with politicians, and business leaders. Some local men, impressed by their methods, flew to Washington to attend the National Prayer Breakfast.

Today, I co-lead a Men's group at my local Church. Incidentally, I finished my paper, written years ago, with the sentence, 'I believe in the importance of men meeting together to support each other is an idea whose time has come'.

> 'God's faithfulness is stronger than our unfaithfulness and our infidelities.'
> POPE FRANCIS

CHAPTER 33

GOD'S RAINDROPS FROM HEAVEN

Over the years our family has experienced times when we were conscious of God's love. I call these 'God's raindrops from heaven'. There have been many. Here are a selected few:

The submissions and appointment of AHMS and SU on the same day. This was the start of Tom Glynn Advertising.

God's Spirit moves in a small country Church. On driving back from seeing my sister Dorothy at Wentworth, NSW, in the late '60s, we attended Church. The preacher was visiting. He was a simple man with a simple sermon of coming to God and receiving a blessing. I've always been suspicious of these altar calls in Churches, but this time it was genuine. Lynda was the first to stand and others followed, including myself, until the whole Congregation was standing - a true revival!

Finding the right therapist. After the frustration of trying to work with two psychiatrists, one appeared at the right time.

Lynda's experience with the death of her parents. Lynda's parents both died on 24 December, seven years apart.

Syd died in 1995 and Rose died in 2002. Syd died at home, in Rose's arms. He had lung cancer. Although Rose was in deep shock and grief and could hardly think straight, she stayed extremely focused on what was to be Syd's last resting place in Salisbury Crematorium Memorial Gardens. The Crematorium kept a Book of Remembrance, open to the current date, where visitors could view short testimonies to their loved ones, which had been organised by themselves earlier. Rose wanted Syd's name and her message of love to him, entered into that book - this was done.

Seven years later, when Rose died, the sisters wondered whether there could possibly be room on that same page, for Rose's name and a message from her family. Surely not, after seven years. Wouldn't the page be filled or another book in its place? They enquired and were overjoyed to learn that there was one more place left on the very same page. So, Rose joined her beloved husband in the same memorial book, on the same page. The sisters added the symbol of a sprig of holly, in remembrance of Syd and Rose's wedding day, at Christmas, on 26 December 1943.

Amazingly, Lynda had spent a long holiday with her parents in the summer, before Syd died unexpectedly a few months later. Likewise, Lynda was with her mother for a holiday, to celebrate Rose's eightieth birthday, the summer before Rose died suddenly at the end of the year. Lynda was grateful to have had that special time with each of her parents just before the end of their lives.

Having spent the summer of 2002 in England, Lynda wanted to stay put in Sydney for a while and delay renewing her passport, which was soon to be out of date, until the new year. But, when

Rose died from a heart attack, she needed to go back to England to attend the funeral and be with her sisters.

Rose died on Christmas Eve and Lynda couldn't fly out until 26 December, Boxing Day. We had a mad scramble to get a new passport for Lynda, including a new passport photo, on a public holiday. However, all things miraculously went well, and we made it to the airport on time.

After Rose's funeral, Lynda and her sisters, Christina and Sheila, had the job of clearing out Rose's house and disposing of her belongings. This was a time of going down memory lane. In many ways, it was a very satisfactory time of closure. Rose had written a beautiful letter, filled with love to her daughters, to be found after she died. She'd divided up her jewellery between her daughters and under many articles in the house, she had put a family member's name, with a kiss from Rose. Lynda, Chris and Sheila found homes for all of Rose's belongings and many keepsakes were given to friends, as well.

When the house looked quite empty, one of the sisters lamented the fact that they had not taken any photos of each room, as they used to be, to have as a reminder of this happy home that we had all loved. Lynda still had a roll of film, from her mother's camera that she had planned to get developed. Lo and behold, as if she'd known, Rose had taken lovely photos of each room in her house and the sisters now had their wish after all.

Meeting interesting characters. There have been a lot of interesting people I have met over the many years I have worked in advertising agencies. It's impossible to mention them all but here are a few:

Graham Wade. The Sydney Morning Herald, in its obituary to the death of Graham Wade on 2 October 2009, headed the article, 'Cartoonist, advertising executive-committed but not cool'. This summed up Graham perfectly. I met him in the early sixties, when he and I created the advertising for the Missouri Australia Crusade. We enjoyed a great friendship, although he became a competitor when he formed Pilgrim Art Studio in 1964. This didn't stop us working together. Graham spoke quickly, rode a bike to work and had a fast brain to solve a creative challenge. One time, he created a cover design for the Anglican Home Mission Society within minutes. To Graham, the message of Christianity, among other things, provided an interesting communication challenge - how to tell such an old story in a new and fresh way? How do you make it as exciting as you found it?

Ramon Williams was a photographer whom we employed to photograph events for our clients. He was a former missionary in Indonesia with the Worldwide Evangelisation Crusade. The mission called for someone to open a new department to produce good quality audio-visuals. On his return he and his wife Dorothy established a company, Worldwide Photos, not only to take photos but to send them to media throughout Australia. I would see Ramon at most Christian functions. He would be in a suit and tie with a few cameras around his neck. A recipient of the prestigious Gutenberg Award, he had interviewed and photographed Mother Teresa. He was also in Darwin after Cyclone Tracy hit on Christmas Eve in December 1974. He admitted he was a workaholic, working from early morning to late every night. Although retired, he now still does the odd photographic assignment. You can't keep a good man down.

Matt Danswan. I met Matt in a Sydney coffee shop in 2003 after he and his wife, Nicole, had recently married, and they had bought what was then a leading Christian magazine, *Alive*, formerly *On Being*. Matt was a keen surfer and the publisher of *Triathlon Monthly*. Later, Matt bought another long-established magazine, *Christian Woman*. TGA was selling advertising space for both magazines. Whilst the magazines had a reasonable circulation, it was difficult to sell space. Religious newspapers and magazines had been greatly impacted by the digital revolution. Matt took over the 'Which' series of Christian guides and the website when I retired. This series, and only a handful of denominational papers, exist today in a printed format. His company, Initiate Media, has grown from a print organisation to a digital operation. Matt has branched out with a book publishing company, Ark House. Over 1,000 books, including this one, have been published by Ark House.

John Smith - God Squad. John Smith founded the God Squad in Sydney in the early '70s to reach a group of Australians not being reached by the Church - motorbike riders. An old friend, Steve Drury, talked me into joining the Board of John's organisation, Care and Communication Concern, in the late eighties. John, himself a bikie, was charismatic with his long hair, jeans and black leather jacket. Steve, his promotional manager, arranged international exposure with concerts in the UK, TV appearances and books that sold in their thousands. In Board meetings in Melbourne, I said the organisation was torn between two conflicting cultures. There was the 'hospital', with the helping of people, and the 'factory', which supported the 'hospital' with effective administration and fundraising. I detected that John was experiencing highs and lows. John knew that I suffered from depression and he admitted he was on the bipolar spectrum. Unlike me, he took no medication because he thought this would dampen his preaching.

John Waterhouse. I regard John as a pioneer of Christian publishing in Australia. He had an interesting career. John graduated from Monash University in 1967. He was a high school teacher in Sabah, East Malaysia, in 1968-1969, and a staff worker for the Scripture Union PNG in 1970-1971. After completing two years at Moore Theological College, John joined the small staff of a regional publishing unit of SU, called ANZEA Publishers. In 1980, he founded Albatross Books. From a staff of one, it grew to a staff of fourteen, with its own premises in Sutherland, Sydney. He published over 200 books. After changes to Australian copyright law, in 1997 he closed his two UK agency agreements - Lion Publishing and IVP (Inter-Varsity Press) - and then his own company in 2000. He served fifteen years on the council of Macarthur Anglican School - nine as chairman.

'Train a child in the way he should go and when he is old he will not turn from it.'
PROVERBS 22:6 NIV

CHAPTER 34

THE GLYNN TRIBE

I was lucky having an older brother Bruce and sister Dorothy - 11 and 8 years respectively.

I was very close to Bruce. He was my mentor and told me to go into advertising. Bruce was possibly a substitute father, before leaving for London when I was twelve years old. He helped me with my schoolwork. He also worked in advertising at McCann's, and retired when he was fifty-eight years old, to live in his 'shack' (as he called it) in Crystal Avenue, Pearl Beach.

He had bought the property in 1964 because of several friends, who were in advertising and had 'weekender' homes there. Over the years, Bruce extended the fibro, one bedroom, house, by adding separate buildings (and then joining them together), because he was worried the local Council would not approve his extensions.

He was an eccentric personality at Pearl Beach. Running a film afternoon at the Progress Hall, he advertised it as a 'Bible Study' to prevent paying for copyright. Bruce screened films from the 1940s, including some of his favourites from that period.

Bruce was also the Santa Claus at Christmas for a few years, before he was sacked for not being genial enough. He carried a bag of sweets for the children, and one woman asked if Santa had any chocolates with soft centres. Bruce told her, 'Who do you think I am, Darryl Lea?' With the death of his partner, Ken Watts, Bruce became increasingly bitter. (I detected depression, which he denied.)

He had a suspicious polyp growing in his bowel and in September 2009 decided to have it removed - against the advice of family and friends, as he suffered from heart trouble. He undertook surgery, which went well. We saw him in hospital before leaving to fly to Phuket on the holiday we had previously booked. We were having a great holiday with our daughter Amanda and her boyfriend, Andy; as well as with our son Steve, his wife Gemma and their children, Oliver and Maya, joining us from their home in Singapore. Andrew proposed to Amanda and we were delighted.

On Wednesday, 30 September, my sister Dorothy phoned to say Bruce had taken a turn for the worse and he died on 1 October 2009. Lynda and I flew home to Sydney and the funeral was held, where over one hundred people attended.

Bruce left his Pearl Beach house to Dorothy and me, and I decided to buy her share. Bruce's death was a shock. Being gay in the 1950s, I believed he hadn't come to terms with his sexuality. On a trip to Europe, he said he didn't enjoy being homosexual. He didn't choose it - and found life difficult. Today, it's all so different.

Lynda and I eventually demolished the house at Pearl Beach and built a new home. I suppose Bruce's time had come.

At seventy-nine, his heart was a worry. He was depressed, withdrawn, and overly concerned with getting old.

My sister Dorothy had at times a sad life. She was married in 1957 to Kevin Mason, a policeman whom she met when she worked as a typist at the NSW Government Garage in Broadway, Sydney. They moved to Bathurst, where Kevin's family lived, and Kevin was attached to the Bathurst Police Station. As well as losing their daughter Karen to a Wilms' tumour (a rare kidney cancer - Karen had the kidney removed when she was four), Kevin and Dorothy also lost their eldest son, Paul Thomas, when, as an air force co-pilot in a helicopter, he crashed into a mountain as part of a routine night exercise in 1978 in South Australia. Five men died. Four were married. Paul, almost 21, was single.

To lose one child is a tragedy, but to lose two children was a major trauma to them both. Sadly, there was no grief counselling, and Kevin threw himself into his work. He finally retired as Chief Inspector at Lithgow Police station in 1988 at the age of fifty-eight. They bought a caravan and travelled around Australia, as well as travelling overseas.

Kevin had a melanoma, for which unfortunately he didn't see a doctor. It developed into a lung cancer and he died in 1995, seven years after retiring. I believed his early death may have been caused by denying and burying his grief and pain, together with working hard, only to find what was buried had arisen in retirement with a tragic result. It's recognised today that what isn't expressed verbally and dealt with can cause physical symptoms. Kevin sought comfort with a country and western song, *'One day at a time sweet Jesus'*.

'How good and pleasant it is when God's people live together in unity!'

PSALM 133:1 NIV

CHAPTER 35

FAMILY MATTERS

Lynda and I have been blessed with our children and grandchildren. Our three children, Michael (born December 1972), Stephen (August 1975) and Amanda (August 1977) enjoyed a happy childhood at our two homes in Roseville.

The birth of a first child is humbling and mystical experience. Lynda was in labour for twenty-five hours before Michael was born at the Royal North Shore Hospital. I stayed most of the time in the waiting room with the other anxious men.

At the start, I was the new boy 'on the block'. As the dads left to see their wife and baby, I gradually moved up finally being the last one, which gave me the opportunity to tell the other men the lay of the land, where the toilets and cafe were and expected waiting time. All based on my almost full day in the waiting room.

Then eventually my time had come. I was ushered in a room with about five people dressed in green and with masks, hovering around Lynda. It looked like they had landed from outer space. I held her hand, rubbed her back and Michael's head appeared. What a moment. Another little person had joined us, crying.

He had ten little fingers and ten little toes! Lynda was exhausted. I phoned my parents and Lynda's parents in England with the good news.

The births of Stephen and Amanda were just as wonderful. I wasn't able to be at their births because I was looking after Michael, and then Stephen as well.

I was not used to childcare. When Amanda was born, I would leave Stephen at the hospital childcare centre, not taking enough nappies and spare clothes for him. When I collected him and Michael from school to visit Lynda, Stephen was dressed in a weird assortment of outfits that the childcare staff had found for him.

Lynda took Michael to England to meet his grandparents. On the nonstop flight to London, Michael crawled into Business Class where Sir Robert Helpmann, famous ballet dancer and actor, was sitting. Sir Robert kindly put his leg out to stop him crawling any further. Michael turned around to return to his Mum.

These were memorable times. Stephen, at age two, climbed into our car, which was parked on a slope in the driveway. He released the hand brake. Lynda was seeing to baby Amanda and from the window, saw the car roll backwards, with Stephen at the wheel! Thankfully, it was stopped by colliding with the neighbours' fence.

When Amanda was about three, she and Stephen and three friends went to watch one of the dads in the neighbourhood paint his garage. He was standing on a ladder, balancing the paint tin on top. The tin toppled, sending paint on to Amanda. The friend's mother, horrified, washed Amanda in the bath, but couldn't remove the brown paint from Amanda's blonde locks. Lynda received a shock and laughed when she saw her new brunette daughter.

I was disappointed that the children didn't have the childhood experiences I had, of playing in bushland, collecting tadpoles and playing with mates until sunset. It was a different time and place.

The children attended Sunday Schools, Girls' and Boys' Brigades and Church house parties. They tell me that they had a happy childhood and never knew I was suffering with clinical depression.

All three did well at school. Michael was a good debater and in the cadets at Barker College. Stephen loved sports. He was captain of the Firsts Basketball team that won the school year's championship. He was also Senior Boy Prefect in his final year. Amanda enjoyed art. She won an award for painting a sad clown. She was a fast runner and became a member of a lively group of girls. They are now respectful, good citizens, married with children.

After leaving school with good results, Michael and Stephen went to the University of NSW. Michael graduated with an Accounting and Finance degree. Stephen was awarded a Co-op scholarship and graduated with a Bachelor of Science (Business Information Technology). Amanda enjoyed her gap year doing interior design. She later worked in marketing and advertising.

Later, the three children travelled overseas to London where Lynda's parents, sisters Sheila and Christine, and their families lived. Michael travelled via South America. He thought he would be one of a few tourists, but was amazed by how many tourists there were. He has now worked at several financial institutions in London, firstly as an accountant and then as a derivative trader.

On what was to be a two-year holiday, like his father, he met Jenny, an accountant, and they married in 2005. I don't believe in the Eastern view of 'Karma', but I reasoned that by taking Lynda to Australia, I had to give up Michael to live in London, where he has been for the past twenty years.

Stephen spent his gap year at Kings Hall College, Taunton, Somerset where, apart from keeping his allocated children in line, he pulled beers at the local pub.

Amanda too, enjoyed her four years in London working as an account executive in top advertising agencies.

I was hoping the children would take over TGA, but none were interested.

Lynda and I were delighted with the choices Michael, Stephen and Amanda made with their marriage partners. Michael married Jenny Singh, youngest daughter of a Guyanese family, who had immigrated to London shortly after she was born. She trained as an accountant and worked at a number of financial institutions in Sydney and London. Stephen married Gemma Dalgleish, previously a lawyer and now a high school teacher. She also worked in a non-profit organisation, Beacon Foundation, helping underprivileged children in remote areas to transition from school to the workforce. They spent nine years in Singapore, where their two children were born. Stephen worked with a number of international banks. Amanda met her husband Andrew at Barker College, where they were in the same year. In my day, they would meet, continue the relationship into their late teens, early twenties, develop a relationship and marry. No, that didn't happen. They went their separate ways and reconnected twelve years later to marry.

Andrew has had an interesting career. After obtaining a degree in Politics and Public Policy, he was advisor to Peter Garrett, the Minister for Arts in Kevin Rudd's ministry. He then worked for several companies as Communications Manager, before studying law in his early thirties. He is now a lawyer with a mid-size law firm in Sydney. Growing up, Andrew spent five years in Washington, D.C. with his mother Nona and father, Richard Palfreyman, an ABC Foreign Correspondent.

Today, Michael works at home as a day trader. Stephen has a senior role with an international company advising large companies on cyber security.

All three families have two children, one a boy, the other a girl. Michael and Jenny have Joseph, now fifteen years and Samira, now thirteen. Stephen and Gemma have Oliver, now thirteen and Maya, now eleven. Amanda and Andrew have Ava, now eight and Jack, now seven.

The grandchildren are a delight. We have been privileged to see the Glynn London family yearly, with holidays in Italy, Spain, Portugal, Thailand, Vietnam, Hong Kong and Singapore. We would drop in to see Stephen and Gemma in Singapore on our returns from London. Stephen jokes he felt unloved because of our short stopovers in Singapore. Incidentally, Michael prefers Mike, Stephen prefers Steve. Amanda is happy being named Amanda. One out of three isn't bad!

'You have been faithful with a few things; I will put you in charge of many things.'
MATTHEW 25:21 NIV

CHAPTER 36

A CHURCH GROWS

In August 2011, I celebrated reaching seventy years of age. Along with our friends, Harvey and Ronnie Gartrell, the family joined Lynda and I at Cape Panwa Hotel in Phuket. I officially retired. But what do I do next? Dad died at seventy-four. Many men then died about five years after retirement. Unlike the previous generation, with medical science, less smoking, and more exercise, meant we could live another fifteen years.

But there was no manual on what to do. No roadmap. Even Freud and Jung had no experiences of the transition from sixty to seventy years of age. I didn't want to play golf, bowls, or tennis, and I was scared I would end up seated in a shopping mall, on a weekday morning, waiting for Lynda to return from shopping, my eyes glazed over with boredom!

Selling our home in Roseville and moving to Watermark Residences for people over fifty-five at nearby Castle Cove, and overseas travel reduced any anxiety. Erikson, the father of life stages, said there were two options for people growing old - stagnation, or 'generativity', giving back and being generous.

I was determined, not to become mean and *bitter* but to be contented and become *better*.

A new avenue of service was moving from Northside Community Church, to a small Baptist Church at St Ives, Sydney. We had spent twenty years at Northside and after I resigned as an Elder, I missed the involvement. Jay Basic had resigned under a cloud of inappropriate behaviour. A new minister, I felt, didn't use my experience in promotion and fundraising. He was an excellent preacher, but I believed he relied more on 'tips and techniques' and introduced more of the praise and worship songs, which would be more at home at Hillsong Church.

So, we stopped attending and travelled overseas for about six months - a spiritual gypsy again.

It's a fact that the largest group of Christians are the lapsed lot, called Christian Alumni - mainly middle aged people who had stopped attending Church because of a range of reasons, including boredom, conflict, or a change in their understanding of their spiritual journey.

It was a new chapter for Lynda and I.

Fortunately, while building a new house at Pearl Beach and selling our home of thirty years at Roseville, I found an advertisement I had kept, published some two years earlier in the local newspaper. It was written by Guy Yeomans from St Ives Baptist Church, offering a Church with a more reflective style of worship.

I found Guy to be an interesting man. He was a teacher, a Liberal member of the NSW Parliament, and had worked in several organisations in a senior role. At the age of thirty-six he went through a mid-life crisis of Faith, discovered Ignatian

A CHURCH GROWS

Spirituality, and then travelled to the USA where he spent six months at a Jesuit retreat centre training to be a Spiritual Director.

Returning to Australia, he joined the team (part time) at Canisius College, a Jesuit retreat centre at Pymble. The nearby St Ives Baptist Church didn't have sufficient funds for a full-time minister, so Guy joined on a three-day basis.

The Church was built in the early 1960s at a time when the population in Sydney's North Shore was growing with young families (similar to East Lindfield Baptist Church). St Ives Baptist Church had seen better days. The huge Sunday School was no longer. The evening service had been discontinued. It had a Congregation of about seventeen people, most of whom were over fifty years of age. Guy said in his report to the Church, 'Unless the Church grows beyond thirty people, we will have to close it!'

On arrival, we found the people friendly. Many were mature Christians and we liked Guy's sermons on spiritual growth. I knew the Church had to grow and I thought there was an opportunity to attract those from the Christian Alumni crowd. The Church website published about these needs.

I wrote a document with several strategies to attract these people. It required an investment of $11,000 to implement the plan, with newspaper advertisements and banners. The money was raised within a few days.

The main recommendation was not new (what is?); I borrowed it from Northside Community Church. It was called, 'Spirited Australians', where well-known Christian people would be interviewed by Guy about their spiritual growth, strengths and weaknesses.

Our first Spirited Australian was Hugh Mackay author and social commentator, in August 2008. We advertised the event with banners, leaflets, posters and newspaper ads. The Service was an outstanding event.

Spirited Australians was based on the concept, not only to inspire our Congregation but to attract people to check us out, knowing there would be others like them at the Service. Since then, almost forty 'Spirited Australians' have appeared. Other notable ones were Geoff Bullock, singer/songwriter, in January 2009 (where there was standing room only), June Dally-Watkins in 2009, Bruce Baird, Federal MP, in 2008, Roger Climpson, former TV presenter, in August 2008, Nick Farr-Jones, former Wallabies Captain, in January 2010 and Lindy Chamberlain in April 2010.

With Lindy, we had no idea that on that day she appeared, in April 2010, it was the thirtieth anniversary of the death of her baby daughter Azariah, taken by a dingo in Central Australia. *The Times*, London, and most of the TV Stations were there. Again, standing room only.

The full list of Spirited Australians is in Appendix 3.

The Church was slowly growing. It didn't have a wide range of programs because of Guy's part-time involvement. Also the older members lacked enthusiasm to start anything new. I was a movie buff (remember the scene of me sticking down film ads when I was eight?) and I introduced a series called, 'God Goes to the Movies', a film I had selected with a religious/spiritual theme was shown. Over a meal with the various courses, we would stop

A CHURCH GROWS

the screening once or twice, to discuss the film. Again, this was popular, and many outstanding films were screened, amongst them *The Shawshank Redemption, Babette's Feast, Chocolat, As It is in Heaven* and *The Mission*.

I also introduced a miniseries of Spirited Australians, called 'An Interesting Life', where I would interview members of the Church. Everyone has a story to tell, but it's sad that not everyone has the opportunity to share it. Sometimes people are afraid that no one will be interested, but they are wrong.

Lynda and I were delighted to be part of a growing and meaningful Church. SIBC knew it couldn't compete with the largest Anglican Church on the North Shore, Christ Church, St Ives, which had a huge number of children and young people. So, we saw ourselves as a niche Church under the slogan 'A Place to Grow Spiritually'. Within ten years and with a new pastor, Rev Beth Jackson, the attendance had grown to over one hundred people, including about fifteen children.

Guy had resigned after ten years to spend time in England with his family, being a pastor to a country Church. We had advertised widely and believed our new minister Beth, was sent from God.

Beth Jackson was born in Kentucky, USA, to Christian parents. She was ordained and worked in England, then worked in Scotland and Europe before coming to Australia with her husband, Darrell. She had been an assistant minister at Epping Baptist Church before coming to St Ives. There are only a handful of female ministers in Baptist Churches in NSW - and Beth is the best!

'Don't just stand there, do something.'
ANONYMOUS

CHAPTER 37

'GET UP' AND 'SPEAK OUT'

In December 2018, with the possibility of a Labor victory making Bill Shorten Prime Minister, a few retired men (a former publisher, politician, company director and a naval officer) together with Guy Yeomans, now returned from the UK and a member at SIBC, as the co-ordinator, all felt that the Church in general and Christians in particular, were being criticised and marginalised in the media. The Church's influence was declining.

A Rugby Union player, Israel Folau, had been sacked for publishing social media content in which he claimed the Bible condemned homosexuals and other people to hell.

Qantas CEO Alan Joyce, himself gay and an advocate for LGBTQI rights, asked Rugby Australia what they were doing to ensure Qantas, a major sponsor, was not reputationally harmed by the controversy. Folau was eventually sacked by Rugby Australia. Although I and the group of retirees did not support the extreme and fundamentalist perspective of Folau's statement, we were disturbed by the growing number of strong-arm tactics to silence freedom of speech, of which his case became a cause celebre.

The motivation to meet was the increasing popularity of 'Get Up' - a large, well-funded organisation with leanings to the left of politics. We felt that Church leaders were impotent, and something had to be done. We created 'Speak Out' - for faith, freedom, family, and our future - and we met with two organisations who may have taken it up, as we didn't have the resources to implement such a task ourselves.

We had raised $60,000 to cover the establishment and copyright of the name, and were confident we could raise $200,000. Unfortunately, the two organisations we approached - The Australian Christian Lobby, Canberra, and Advance Australia, Brisbane - turned us down.

However, the May 2019 election saw the Liberals returned to power with Scott Morrison, a self-professed Christian, elected as Prime Minister. Negativity against the Church and Christians had been halted in some places. 'Get Up' influence had been greatly reduced. The media discovered that people of Faith - Christians, Jews, Muslims, Hindus and Buddhists - were much larger and influential than they had previously thought.

'You are never too old to set another goal or dream a new dream.'
C. S. LEWIS

CHAPTER 38

NOW WHAT?

As I approach eighty years of age, I review my life, family, friends, struggles and successes. In my professional life, my purpose had been to bring advertising/modern marketing insights and skills to Christian causes, which has been achieved. As one of the first agencies to specialise in fundraising, I was encouraged when the Fundraising Institute Australia was established in 1972 with thirty members. FIA was successful in creating a new industry of professional fundraising people.

Also, tertiary organisations were teaching students marketing/advertising, and many joined Christian causes. The Commonwealth and State Governments were directing their funds to charities, thus increasing the number of people working in not-for-profit groups.

Indeed, the largest employer in Australia is the Christian Church, made up through hospitals, schools, retirement homes and welfare charities.

However, these Christian organisations, over the years, have tried to attract staff with a Church/Christian background. Unfortunately, this availability is drying up, forcing the charities to employ staff with only a stated commitment to the values of the charity's standards and ethics.

Furthermore, Church going is declining. Entry points for people have gone. These were Sunday Schools, Boys' and Girls' Brigades, Youth Fellowships and Vacation Bible Schools. Also articulate ministers, who were able to present the Christian message through the media, have gone. Sadly, they are not being replaced.

In my lifetime, various expressions of Faith have been:
The House or Home Church
The Liberation Movement
The Healing Ministry
Charismatic Renewal Movement
Signs and Wonders
Small Groups
The Emerging Church
Mega Churches
Ethnic-based Churches
Seeker-sensitive Services
Alpha Groups

Religious sects have come and gone. In theology there has been a huge shift. Many evangelicals believe in a personal Faith that Jesus died to earn us a place in heaven. For me, sin and hell have been replaced by God's grace, love and forgiveness. The original curse in Genesis has been replaced, in some places, as an original blessing. The punitive gospel or sin management, which provides believers with the hope of heaven, 'pie in the sky when you die', is receding.

However, some Christian authors and theologians are becoming more popular. These include Richard Rohr, a Franciscan priest, from the Centre for Action and Contemplation, USA, Matthew Fox (*Original Blessing*), Brian McLaren, writer of the *Emerging Church*, and N. T. Wright, former Anglican Bishop of Durham, UK, among others.

But, to the average Australian, Christianity is not relevant to them. Heaven is now. Science and humanism have helped create a secular culture. And articulate atheists are writing books that are selling well.

In fact, many Australians are indifferent, while some are critical of the Church, because of sexual misconduct among the clergy and the Church's attitude to sex. The 2019 legislation of marriage equality is still opposed by many people of Faith.

However, one good sign. Christianity in Asia and South America is growing. It is said that there will be more Christians in China than in the USA in ten years. The current persecution of Chinese Christians and the destruction of Churches will quite possibly have the opposite result and lead to a rise in Christianity.

During the crisis and impact of the COVID19 pandemic, research has shown more people are praying and seeking methods of spirituality-like mindfulness. The outcome is uncertain. But the virus is and will have a big impact on all of us into the future.

Mental health issues are being discussed more now, at a time with disturbing increase in suicide. I was reluctant to talk about my depression for many years, until I realised that some one in four people will suffer from a mental illness during their lives. By sharing my experience with others, I hope it will help this discussion.

The motivation to excel and be financially secure was developed in my younger years. In working for myself, I was a commander and control freak. I was successful in our recommendations for clients, which should have led to confidence, but I think it was expressed in arrogance. I thought I knew it all, and was pushy, goal directed, selfish, and motivated to please.

At forty years of age, I discovered that not everyone sees life as I see it! Rejection was my unpleasant motivation to do something. 'Don't just stand there, do something!' My need to excel led me to read self-help books. I've learnt instead of doing, to be; instead of talking, to listen; instead of cursing, to bless; and instead of anger, to accept.

My egotism must be acknowledged and reduced. Let things happen through me, not by me! Letting go of things past is a good thing. I am trying to let go of the past, which is holding me back to live a more satisfying and enjoyable life. As St Paul wrote in his Letter to the Philippians 3:13, 'But one thing I do: forgetting what is behind and straining toward what is ahead'. I also try to avoid 'toxic' people, who I find negative and unpleasant.

Lynda and I enjoy spending time at retreat centres with spiritual directors to help us on the Christian journey.

Work has been a big part of my life. For many people, the workplace is unsatisfactory and permits neither growth nor creativity. Often, it is an anonymous place where function and image have control. Since work demands such labour and effort, it has always made the worker vulnerable. It's even more so today with little job security, high redundancy rates and limited career opportunities.

NOW WHAT?

I was blessed. I loved my work. When struggling with life and depression, I reminded myself that I had a job I enjoyed. Even retiring at seventy five, I still had time for creative projects, as a Deacon at my Church. Writing this book has been exciting.

There have been many changes in advertising. When I started working there were only two international advertising agencies in Australia - J. Walter Thompson and Lintas in Sydney. All others, on the whole, were named after individuals. The scene changed in 1958 when McCann Erickson from New York took over Hanson Rubensohn. Others followed. Jackson Wain, where I spent my twenties, was taken over in 1970 by Leo Burnett, Chicago.

Talking of changes, there have been many changes in advertising agencies since I joined R. S. Maynard in 1957.

1) **More women.** Secretaries and a few copy writers have been supported by women in account management roles.

2) **Technology.** The Mac revolution moved artists from drawing on a board to drawing on a screen. It expanded the number of graphic artists. Everyone with a Mac computer saw themselves as an artist.

3) **Social media.** TV, radio and commercials, newspapers, outdoor and magazine adverts were once the only media selected by advertisers. Now, social media platforms have increased their share of advertisers' media budgets.

4) **Media buying services.** Agencies once had their own media departments who selected and booked the

media. Today, most agencies use exterior media buying services.

5) **Loss of agency commission and service fees.** The standard 10% paid to accredited agencies has gone, along with the service fee. Today, fees are negotiated.
6) **Mergers.** The big are getting bigger. Long established agencies are gone, replaced by giant holding companies. George Patterson and JWT Australia are no more.
7) **Lack of client loyalty.** Once, the client and agency were partners. Today, many clients regard agencies as another provider. A new client executive believes changing his agency will enhance his or her career.
8) **Professional training.** Most people entering advertising agencies have been to University.

I have also seen many changes with our clients. Anglican Home Mission Society became Home Mission Society (HMS) and now Anglicare, merging with Anglican Retirement Villages. They had a ministry up to the late 70s at Wahroonga called Carramar, where young pregnant girls and women could live before their baby arrived. Another Anglican agency would help in the adoption of the baby. We advertised Carramar in *Dolly*, a magazine directed to teenage girls. Baptist Community Care (BCS) became Baptist Care.

Today, Lynda and I spend half a week at Pearl Beach and half a week at Watermark. We love travelling. I often say, 'If I died tomorrow, I would die a happy man'. I've had a wonderful career in advertising and my lifelong goal has been achieved. We have three great children and six lovely grandchildren. We have enough to live on, and I'm healthy for my age. Hopefully, I don't think I'll have to rent a crowd for my funeral. God has been good. Jesus a friend. The Holy Spirit an encourager.

I have compiled my funeral service, which will include this poem:

> *'When you were born you were crying*
> *and everyone else was smiling.*
> *Live your life*
> *so, at the end,*
> *you are the one who is smiling*
> *and everyone else is crying.'*
> *Ralph Waldo Emerson*

APPENDIX 1

AGENCIES AND CLIENTS

R. S. Maynard Sydney: Commercial Banking Company of Sydney, Lloyd Triestino Shipping Co.

Jackson Wain Sydney: Australian Dairy Produce Board, White Wings, Akubra Hats, Sunbeam

Jackson Wain Singapore: Australian Dairy Produce Board, Qantas, Proctor and Gamble, Horlicks, Sampson luggage, Malaysian Singapore Airlines

Hobson Bates & Partners London: British American Tobacco, British Travel, World Advertising Conference

J. Walter Thompson Sydney: Bonds Clothing, Lever & Kitchen, Pan Am, John Lysaght

Tom Glynn Advertising Sydney: Thomas Organs, Mills and Boon, Golden Press, Building Societies of NSW, HomeWorld, Bain Dawes, AWA, Borg Warner, Repco plus others

APPENDIX 2

TGA HAS ENJOYED THE PRIVILEGE OF WORKING WITH THESE CHRISTIAN ORGANISATIONS:

- ACOM - Australian College of Ministries
- ALIVE Magazine
- Anglicare/Anglican Home Mission Society
- Australian Council of Churches (Christmas Bowl)
- Baptist Community Services/Baptist Care
- Baptist Union of NSW
- Baptist Union of Queensland
- Bible Society
- Bush Church Aid Society
- Campus Crusade for Christ/ Power to Change
- Catholic Mission
- Christian Woman Magazine
- Church Resources
- Churches of Christ
- CMS-Church Missionary Society
- Communicare/Integricare
- Compassion
- Hope Healthcare
- NSW Council of Churches
- Scripture Union
- Sydney Anglican Schools Corporation
- Sydney City Mission
- Wesley Mission

APPENDIX 3

SPIRITED AUSTRALIAN SPEAKERS

Hugh Mackay - Social Commentator
Dr Phil Siddal - Pain specialist RNSH
Bruce Baird - former Federal MP
Geoff Bullock - Singer/Songwriter
Mark Scott - CEO of the ABC
June Dally-Watkins - former Model
Roger Climpson - former TV Presenter
Dr Cliff Powell - Clinical Psychologist
Fred Kong - former CEO, Richmond Fellowship
Nick Farr-Jones - former Wallabies Captain
Lindy Chamberlain - survivor of legal injustice
Roy Williams - Lawyer, journalist & author
David & John Ayliffe - survivors of a cult
Roger Corbett - former CEO of Woolworths
Brian Howe - former Deputy Prime Minister
Tony Kevin - former Ambassador, 'Walking the Camino'
Ewan Crouch - Chairman of partners, Allens Law Firm
Dr Ern Crocker - Nuclear medicine specialist
Dr Briony Scott - Principal of Wenona School
Greg Smith - NSW Attorney General
Dr Karen and Dr Perry Shaw - Middle East perspectives

Dr Mike Pope - Meteorologist
Dr Tim Hawkes - Headmaster of King's School
Azim and Pouye - refugees from Iran
A/Professor Andrew Cole - Chief Medical Officer, Greenwich Hospital
Megan Krimmer - Principal of Roseville College
Bob Ellicott QC - Solicitor General, Judge
A/Prof Peter Achterstraat - former Auditor General and Deputy Tax Commissioner
Prof Alanna Nobbs - Professor in Ancient History Macquarie University
Rev Graham Long - Pastor & CEO, Wayside Chapel
Rabbi Gad Krebs - Kehillat Masada Synagogue, St Ives
Paul Fletcher MP - Federal member for Bradfield
Dr Jim Greenwood - A/Prof of Psychiatry and co-founder of Black Dog Institute
Lyn Worsley - Clinical psychologist
Andrew Scipione - former NSW Police Commissioner
Dr Andrew Sloane - GP and Morling College lecturer
Robert Grant AO - former Headmaster, Shore School

For media, events, interviews and speaking events, please contact Tom:
tjglynn@outlook.com

www.tomglynn-godsadman.com.au
www.tomglynn.com.au

Mum and Dad, before they married.

Dad's family. Dad, seventh from the left, behind Grandma and Grandpop Glynn.

Tom, aged 13 with Mum and Dad.

Mum and Dad, on holiday at Saratoga, NSW.

Tom, aged 13 at Petersham.

Tom, now an Ad-Man.

Singapore. Advertising photographic session with models.

Samsonite luggage advertisement.

Tom, a model for a client advertisement.

Wedding, 21st October 1967 at Saint Lawrence's Church, Old Sarum, Salisbury, UK.

Honeymoon, Majorca, Spain.

European coach tour.

Lynda's parents, Syd and Rose Wyatt, Salisbury, UK.

Syd in uniform.

Bonds presentation. From left: John Adams, Tom, Ken Done and model.

First day at Tom Glynn Advertising

Liberace shoot in the garage of his mansion. From right: Alan Dickes – director, Ross Meillon – creative director, both partially hidden behind leaves.

Move to bigger premises flyer in 1974. From left: Tom, Ross Meillon – creative director, Jenny McBride – artist, Christen Zara – secretary.

Anglican Home Mission Society film shoot. From left: Ross Meillon – creative director, Roger Climpson, Alan Dickes – director.

Family at Pearl Beach NSW, From left: Dorothy Mason – sister, Bruce Glynn – brother, Stephen Glynn, Amanda Glynn, Michael Glynn, Lynda Glynn, Ken Watts.

Lunch to celebrate ten years of TGA.

Ken Watts and Bruce Glynn.

Bruce at home at Pearl Beach.

From left: Tom Glynn, Mike South from Mills & Boon and Abe Luyben from TGA.

An unsuccessful concept.

Which Christian Guides and website.

Speak Out! advertisement.

Family cruise in 2018.

www.ingramcontent.com/pod-product-compliance
Lightning Source LLC
Chambersburg PA
CBHW070554100426
42744CB00006B/276